Dvořák

Unlocking the Masters Series, No. 5

Dvořák

Romantic Music's
Most Versatile Genius

David Hurwitz

AMADEUS
PRESS

Published in 2005 by

Amadeus Press, LLC
512 Newark Pompton Turnpike
Pompton Plains, New Jersey 07444, USA

For sales, please contact

NORTH AMERICA

AMADEUS PRESS, LLC
c/o Hal Leonard Corp.
7777 West Bluemound Road
Milwaukee, Wisconsin 53213, USA
Phone: 800-637-2852
Fax: 414-774-3259

E-mail: orders@amadeuspress.com
Website: www.amadeuspress.com

UNITED KINGDOM AND EUROPE

ROUNDHOUSE PUBLISHING LTD.
Millstone, Limers Lane
Northam, North Devon EX39 2RG, UK
Phone: 01237-474474
Fax: 01237-474474
E-mail: roundhouse.group@ukgateway.net

Printed in Canada

Library of Congress Cataloging-in-Publication Data

Hurwitz, David, 1961–
    Dvořák : romantic music's most versatile genius / by David Hurwitz.
       p. cm. — (Unlocking the masters series ; no. 5)
    ISBN 1-57467-107-3
    1. Dvořák, Antonín, 1841–1904—Criticism and interpretation. I. Title. II. Series.
ML410.D99H84 2005
780'.92—dc22

                                    2005013243

This book is dedicated with love to my grandmother,
Ethel Hurwitz, for her constant faith and support.

Contents

Acknowledgments

This book received a great deal of encouragement and support from a whole host of friends and colleagues. First, I need to thank Graham Melville-Mason at The Dvořák Society for Czech and Slovak Music for his useful suggestions, as well as Professor Jan Smaczny at Queen's University, Belfast, who so kindly shared with me some of his thoughts on Dvořák's operas (*Alfred* in particular).

I am also indebted to numerous colleagues who listened endlessly to my "discoveries" and ideas about Dvořák and his music, particularly Sören Meyer-Eller, Christophe Huss, David Vernier, Karl Schuster, Victor Carr Jr., Barry Guerrero, and most of all, my editor Bob Levine, who just may have come around to loving some of the operas as much as I do despite their being in Czech. I'm sure all will be relieved to know that their subscriptions to the "Daily Dvořák" have finally expired.

I also wish to extend my appreciation to Bärenreiter Praha for help in sourcing many of the scores. I hope that the new critical edition proceeds swiftly and successfully under their watchful auspices. Special thanks also to Supraphon Records, and to Jana Gonda.

A Note on the Music

Opus numbers are sometimes useful in identifying Dvořák's works but almost worthless in dating them. This is because Dvořák's publisher, Simrock, much to the composer's irritation, placed high numbers on early pieces so that people would think they were new. The fact that this worked gives ample proof of the excellence of much early Dvořák, but it makes the dating of his music look very strange indeed. The composer, by the same token, annoyed at being shortchanged by his publisher, back-opused (if I may invent the term) some later works so that he could claim they predated his exclusive contract with Simrock and thus sell them to other publishers. Later he abandoned even this tactic and told Simrock, in so many words, "So sue me." That never happened, but rest assured that the dates given are correct, as are those opus numbers that I find it useful to include.

Regarding my approach in general, Dvořák's knowledge and experience of Western musical culture, as well as his later impact on it, is in my view significantly greater than is often supposed. For that reason, you will find many other composers and their works mentioned in the following pages. It may not be possible to pin down the exact amount of each ingredient in Dvořák's own musical "secret recipe," but that doesn't mean that one can't or shouldn't try to describe its complex and seductive blend of flavors. However, I want to be very clear that you do not need to know all this other music in order to enjoy or understand Dvořák. Each of his works speaks for itself. I include these references because of their intrinsic relevance, and also so that you may use this book as a guide to new listening experiences, including the music and musicians that he heard, learned from, and possibly influenced.

Every major work of Dvořák is mentioned here. I have omitted for reasons of space some piano pieces, songs, and lesser choral works, as well as a few brief chamber and orchestral items. As it is, more than ninety individual compositions are discussed, many at length, and the accompanying CDs offer more than twenty listening selections, each one described in detail. I have also included a timeline placing Dvořák in his context chronologically, noting when his major works were written as compared to those of his most important contemporaries. This is both interesting and helpful in getting your bearings concerning an enormously varied and productive period in musical history. In all other respects, I believe the organization and layout of the book pose no special problems, and you can read it in order or dip into it at will.

Dvořák Timeline

Approximate Date of Composition/Premiere/Publication

Year	Selected Major Works by Dvořák	Contemporary Musical Landmarks
1841	Dvořák born	Adam: *Giselle*
1846		Berlioz conducts his music in Prague
1853		Verdi: *Il Trovatore; La Traviata*
1854		Wagner: *Tannhäuser* (Prague premiere); Berlioz: *L'Enfance du Christ*
1856		Wagner: *The Flying Dutchman; Lohengrin* (Prague premieres); Schumann dies
1858		Berlioz: *Les Troyens*
1859		Brahms: Piano Concerto No. 1
1860		Mahler born
1861	String Quintet No. 1	Brahms: Piano Quartet No. 1
1862	String Quartet No. 1	Verdi: *La forza del destino;* Smetana: *The Brandenburgers in Bohemia;* Liszt: *The Legend of St. Elizabeth*
1863		Wagner conducts his music in Prague
1864		Smetana conducts Berlioz: *Roméo et Juliette*

Year	Selected Major Works by Dvořák	Contemporary Musical Landmarks
1865	Symphonies Nos. 1 and 2	Schubert:"Unfinished" Symphony (1st perf.); Wagner: *Tristan und Isolde* (1st perf.)
1866		Bruckner: Symphony No. 1; Tchaikovsky: Symphony No. 1; Smetana: *The Bartered Bride* (first version); Smetana conducts Liszt: *The Legend of St. Elizabeth*
1867		Wagner: *Die Meistersinger;* Liszt: *Christus*
1868		Smetana: *Dalibor*
1869	String Quartets Nos. 2 and 3	Brahms: Hungarian Dances, books 1 and 2
1870	String Quartet No. 4; *Alfred*	Tchaikovsky: *Romeo and Juliet;* Wagner: *Siegfried-Idyll*
1871		Verdi: *Aida;* Wagner: *Siegfried; Die Meistersinger* (Prague premiere)
1872	Piano Quintet No. 1; *The Heirs of the White Mountain;* Symphony No. 3	Tchaikovsky: Symphony No. 2; Mussorgsky: *Boris Godunov;* Smetana: *Libuse*
1873	String Quartets Nos. 5 and 6	Brahms: *Variations on a Theme by Haydn;* String Quartets Nos. 1 and 2
1874	Symphony No. 4; Symphonic Poem (Rhapsody) in A Minor; String Quartet No. 7; *The King and the Charcoal Burner; The Stubborn Lovers*	Bruckner: Symphony No. 4; Wagner: *Götterdämmerung;* Verdi: Requiem

Year	Selected Major Works by Dvořák	Contemporary Musical Landmarks
1875	Symphony No. 5; Serenade for Strings; String Quintet No. 2 ("Double Bass"); Piano Trio No. 1; Piano Quartet No. 1; *Vanda;* Moravian Duets	Bizet: *Carmen;* Smetana: *Má Vlast* (Nos. 1 and 2); Verdi: *Aida* (Prague premiere)
1876	Piano Trio No. 2; String Quartet No. 8; Theme and Variations, for solo piano; Piano Concerto	Brahms: Symphony No. 1; Smetana: String Quartet No. 1
1877	Serenade for Winds; String Quartet No. 9; *The Cunning Peasant;* Stabat Mater; Symphonic Variations	Brahms: Symphony No. 2
1878	Slavonic Dances I; Slavonic Rhapsodies; Bagatelles, for string trio and harmonium; String Sextet in A	Brahms: Violin Concerto; Tchaikovsky: Symphony No. 4; *Eugene Onegin*
1879	*Czech Suite;* String Quartet No. 10; *Silhouettes,* for piano; Violin Concerto	Smetana: *Má Vlast* (completed)
1880	Symphony No. 6; Violin Sonata; *Gypsy Melodies*	Brahms: Hungarian Dances, books 3 and 4; Bizet: *Carmen* (Prague premiere)
1881	*Legends;* String Quartet No. 11; *My Home Overture*	Offenbach: *Tales of Hoffman;* Brahms: Piano Concerto No. 2; Tchaikovsky: Serenade for Strings
1882	*Dimitrij*	Wagner: *Parsifal*
1883	Scherzo Capriccioso; *Hussite Overture;* Piano Trio No. 3	Brahms Symphony No. 3; Wagner dies
1884	*From the Bohemian Forest,* for piano duet; *The Specter's Bride*	Massenet: *Manon*

Year	Selected Major Works by Dvořák	Contemporary Musical Landmarks
1885	Symphony No. 7	Brahms: Symphony No. 4; Wagner: *Das Rheingold; Die Walküre* (Prague premieres); Grieg: *Holberg Suite,* for strings
1886	*St. Ludmila*	Liszt dies; Saint-Saëns: Organ Symphony; Wagner: *Tristan und Isolde* (Prague premiere)
1887	Slavonic Dances II; Terzetto in C, for two violins and viola; Romantic Pieces, for violin and piano; *Cypresses,* for string quartet; Piano Quintet No. 2; Mass in D	Brahms: Double Concerto; Verdi: *Otello*
1888	*The Jacobin*	Tchaikovsky: Symphony No. 5; *Sleeping Beauty;* Franck: Symphony in D Minor
1889	Symphony No. 8; Piano Quartet No. 2; *Poetic Tone Pictures*, for piano	Mahler: Symphony No. 1; Strauss: *Don Juan; Death and Transfiguration*
1890	Requiem	Tchaikovsky: *The Queen of Spades*
1891	*In Nature's Realm; Carnival;* "Dumky" Trio	Carnegie Hall opens
1892	*Othello;* Te Deum	Leoncavallo: *I Pagliacci;* Massenet: *Werther*
1893	Symphony No. 9; String Quintet No. 3; Sonatina in G, for violin and piano; *The American Flag;* String Quartet No. 12 ("American")	Verdi: *Falstaff;* Tchaikovsky dies; Symphony No. 6 "Pathétique"

Year	Selected Major Works by Dvořák	Contemporary Musical Landmarks
1894	Humoresques, for piano; *Biblical Songs*	Mahler: Symphony No. 2
1895	Cello Concerto; "American" Suite; String Quartets Nos. 13 and 14	Strauss: *Till Eulenspiegel's Merry Pranks*
1896	*The Water Goblin; The Noon Witch; The Wood Dove; The Golden Spinning Wheel*	Mahler: Symphony No. 3; Puccini: *La Bohème;* Bruckner dies
1897	*Heroic Song*	Brahms dies; Strauss: *Don Quixote*
1898		Strauss: *Ein Heldenleben*
1899	*The Devil and Kate*	Sibelius: Symphony No. 1; Elgar: *Enigma Variations*
1900	*Rusalka*	Mahler: Symphony No. 4; Puccini: *Tosca*
1901		Verdi dies
1902		Mahler: Symphony No. 5; Debussy: *Pelléas et Mélisande*
1903	*Armida*	Sibelius: Violin Concerto
1904	Dvořák dies	Puccini: *Madama Butterfly*

Dvořak

Dvořák in Focus

The music of Antonin Dvořák defies fashion. He is one of the very few composers whose works entered the international mainstream during his own lifetime, and some of them have remained there ever since. You would probably be surprised to learn just how rare an occurrence this is. Reputations tend to wax and wane with the times. Dvořák's case is different. He never had to be discovered by future generations (as did Bach and Mahler), nor did he suffer a drastic eclipse in the performance of his most famous works (as happened to Sibelius). On the other hand, the pieces that historically define his international reputation represent only a small fraction of what he actually composed. They comprise just one facet of his complex and remarkably rich artistic personality.

Even more strangely, his frequency of performance and recording, what one might call Dvořák's "real-word esteem," often coexists simultaneously with a strikingly condescending view both of the man himself and much of his music: the hugely popular as well as the unfamiliar. Until recordings made the bulk of his output generally available to music lovers, no hard evidence existed to challenge these skeptical views of his art. There was little inducement to try to see his creative personality whole—never mind opportunities to encourage new encounters with a body of barely known works—despite the fact that, once heard, many of them appear not to have deserved their relative neglect. Indeed, if one defines *greatness* as the ability to create a series of masterpieces over a broad range of musical media, then Dvořák was, demonstrably and without exaggeration, the greatest composer of the last half of the nineteenth century.

Not that the field was all that crowded. Dvořák only had serious competition from three others in the "generalist" category: Saint-Säens, Brahms, and Tchaikovsky—the last two unquestionably great in various ways, the first a composer ripe for reevaluation but one who, as of now, simply lacks the standing of his more illustrious colleagues in every genre in which he worked. Certainly Tchaikovsky was Dvořák's equal as a writer for the orchestra, but on the other hand, chamber music never occupied a significant place in the Russian composer's creative life. Brahms, most would concede, was a master in every medium that he attempted, but his orchestral output (however distinguished) is small, and he never bothered with opera or other forms of music for the stage. Only Dvořák offers maximum variety while maintaining a remarkably high level of excellence across the board, and in quantity.

Certainly not all his music is of uniform quality: no one's is. Bach had his share of perfunctory church cantatas. Beethoven wrote the dull Triple Concerto, the justly neglected oratorio *Christ on the Mount of Olives*, and the uninspired Mass in C. Few care about Tchaikovsky's Second Piano Concerto or Third Symphony, nor do many people maintain that Brahms's string quartets rise to the level of his finest chamber works with piano. Or consider *Rinaldo*, the major choral work of his entire career next to the *German Requiem* and essentially forgotten today. In all these cases, the composer's mastery in his best pieces overcomes any reservations that listeners might encounter during their stroll down the broad path of enjoyment. So it is with Dvořák, whose weaknesses (as you will see) are as obvious as they have proven unimportant to his best music's durability and seemingly perpetual freshness.

However, as with all prolific composers, any appreciation of Dvořák's total output necessarily takes lots of time. This applies especially to the neglected operas and extended choral works, where it's always easier to make fun of silly librettos or criticize the notes on the page (often according to inappropriate stylistic criteria) than it is to actually listen to what the composer wrote. Dvořák has endured more than his share of this kind of lazy criticism. Even more damaging, because of the genuine barriers to appreciation of his work that they pose, are certain half-baked views concerning his personality and working habits, originating in his own lifetime, which have been handed down ever since. Many of these arose as a consequence of nineteenth-century nationalism, a poisonous intellectual brew whose political manifestations have long been discredited thanks to a couple of world wars and the defeat of fascism, but whose cultural legacy remains very much with us where music is concerned. This significant topic, perhaps the defining intellectual current in Dvořák's creative life, is best viewed in terms of the light it sheds on various individual works.

However, it had one very important offshoot that needs addressing up front: the slanted perception of his friendship with Brahms. This artistically momentous relationship began with Brahms's support of Dvořák's application for an Austrian state grant in 1875 and continued a couple of years later with his recommendation of Dvořák to Simrock, his Berlin publisher. From these generous acts, a friendship between the two gradually developed, spurred on by genuine mutual admiration. Nevertheless, overviews of the two men's musical interaction often take some form of this (admittedly extreme) formulation: Brahms was a worldly, urban sophisticate working in the glorious German musical tradition, while the younger (by eight years)

Dvořák, of racially inferior peasant stock from the Czech provinces, was essentially a naïve country bumpkin with a knack for writing good tunes but otherwise possessed of scant intellectual resources. He was successful to the extent that he followed the advice and example of Brahms, and a failure to the degree that he unwisely attempted to pursue an independent path (or even worse, Wagner's).

The more you come to know Dvořák's music, the stranger this viewpoint will seem. Brahms certainly never saw him that way, despite a strong streak of German nationalism that today would be called bigotry, and his friendship was much more than mere charity. Consider, for example, the following facts in light of the "Dvořák Timeline" of major works. The Sixth Symphony (1880) is widely considered derivative of Brahms's Second (1877). There's no question that Dvořák knew the Brahms and admired it very much. But the alleged influence hangs on two flimsy pieces of evidence: both symphonies share the key of D major, and both have finales that begin with a flowing, quiet theme for the full string section. Beyond that, there's no significant similarity worth mentioning. In fact, the Czech composer had five remarkable symphonies under his belt before Brahms even published his first.

Now turn the argument around: examine the possibility that Brahms's Third Symphony (1883) borrows certain significant features from Dvořák's Fifth (1875). Both symphonies share the same key (F major); the introduction to Dvořák's scherzo and the main tune of the symphony's slow movement, for cellos, are both similar in scoring and mode to the theme that opens Brahms's third movement. Dvořák puts his finale in a minor key, which is very unusual in a symphony that opens in the major, and so does Brahms. The earlier work daringly (for its time) refers back to the opening theme of the first movement just before the end, and so does the Brahms. Most important, Brahms's woodwind writing in the first movement's second thematic group and much of the slow movement sounds amazingly like Dvořák's. Indeed, the evidence for Brahms doing the conceptual copying here is far more compelling than the converse, but you will almost never hear anyone dare make such a suggestion.

The reality, of course, is that all such theories, when used for anything other than purely academic purposes, demean both composers, particularly to the extent that they deny the obvious fact that artists always seize on whatever material they need to make their expressive points. What matters is not the source of the inspiration but what ultimately gets made of it. In this case, each composer had something that the other could use. Brahms offered unsurpassed formal mastery allied to a brilliant and scholarly intellect. Dvořák had immense practical experience as an orchestral musician, a genuine gift at scoring, and an inexhaustible fund of superb musical ideas. If Brahms perhaps helped Dvořák to express himself more cogently without inhibiting his effusive melodic inspiration, then Dvořák similarly encouraged Brahms to color his music more vividly without compromising its basic economy of means. It was, in short, a wholly productive relationship, supportive of each artist's conscious effort to write great music of universal appeal in his own personal style.

The natural affinity that grew up between the two men (who only actually met in person a handful of times) appears even less puzzling if one compares their respective origins, for here too they had much in common. Dvořák, it has to be stressed, was *not* a peasant, if by this one means a subsistence farmer tied to the land. He was the son of a village innkeeper and butcher. His father was also a good enough musician to play the zither and the violin at least semiprofessionally, and his family, while taking care to insist that he learn his father's trade, was supportive of his musical career. Brahms's paternal grandfather was, like Dvořák's dad, a country innkeeper, and his father was a double-bass player who married his maid. Brahms received his basic musical education in Hamburg (population in 1850: 132,000); Dvořák in Prague (population in 1850: 118,000), a city at least as important as a regional (and former imperial) capital and just as rich culturally. The country vs. city dichotomy is, in any case, almost invariably exaggerated by modern writers forgetful of the fact that a typical urban residence in the nineteenth century differed in few significant ways from a rural homestead, right down to the stables.

In order to achieve broad acceptance as a serious composer, Dvořák faced a unique set of problems. An extremely strong national identity in music was a two-edged sword in a world steeped in cultural and racial stereotypes. Although extremely patriotic and proud of his heritage, he wanted his music to be understood as great art generally, not as a mere exotic curiosity, and he would be damned before being known as "the Czech Brahms." So he used the term "Slavonic" to describe his efforts in a purportedly nationalist idiom, and he adopted Polish, Ukrainian, Russian, and even (in one piano piece) Scottish dance forms and rhythms to universalize his own brand of ethnic music. In his operas, he enjoyed paying the necessary homage to the rustic village comedies popularized by Smetana, but when it came to larger historical dramas, he placed them in England (*Alfred*), Poland (*Vanda*) and Russia (*Dimitrij*), enlarging his expressive reach by looking beyond his native frontiers.

Both composers found common cause in putting their respective musical languages to work in the service of the classical forms and genres that they revered above all others. Their fundamental goal lay in achieving the perfect balance of emotion and intellect, of the popular and the erudite that defined the first great Viennese school of composers—Haydn, Mozart, and Beethoven. Brahms deliberately spent his entire life reaffirming the ongoing vitality of classical-period forms and musical syntax, and he was undoubtedly this style's last great exponent. Dvořák seems to have been more pragmatic in his view. He reserved the Viennese classical style for those pieces that he thought required its use, and he firmly believed in mastering the idiom for just that purpose. However, it remained but one tool (albeit a very major one) in his artistic arsenal.

Another quick glance at the timeline shows that in Dvořák's case, even this last, classicizing trait was firmly in place well before he could have encountered many of Brahms's major works (that is, prior to the premiere of the latter's First Symphony in 1876). The stylistic curve of the first five symphonies alone proves this conclusively. This does not diminish the importance of the older composer in Dvořák's life, but rather puts into perspective exactly what role Brahms may have played in helping him realize his musical ambitions in those areas where their interests converged. One thing is certain: they really liked each other's music. Dvořák orchestrated some of Brahms's Hungarian Dances, and Brahms was happy to edit for European publication the Ninth Symphony ("From the New World")—and much else besides—when Dvořák was still busy teaching in America. Like Haydn and Mozart, they seemed to enjoy a companionship completely without envy, perhaps borne of a certainty, not only that their talents were complementary and in no way mutually exclusive, but also that they were the two finest composers around and therefore members of a very special club.

Even so, their admiration was not uncritical: Brahms raised an eyebrow or two at Dvořák's formal liberties and occasional lack of concision, and as for Dvořák—in later life he abandoned the symphony entirely in favor of the symphonic poems and operas being produced by the much-despised (by musical conservatives) Liszt/Wagner camp. Naturally he did this for his own good reasons, but Brahms partisans have never quite forgiven him for this perceived betrayal. Unfortunately, they were also the same folks largely responsible for the music-history books and musicological studies of the past century or so. As a result of their cultural biases, it is accepted as given that Brahms and Wagner were irreconcilable aesthetic opposites, so much so that the very notion that the same person (and a non-German at that) could compose both excellent symphonies and fine operas remains all but unthinkable even today. Yet this is exactly what Dvořák did.

Brahms's single-mindedness of purpose is taken for granted and admired unreservedly. Why then is Dvořák, who certainly matched or even exceeded Brahms in sheer talent and determination, seldom afforded the same respect, simply because he failed to accept the constraints that the cultural stereotypes of his time sought to impose on him? Or more precisely, why has it taken so long to accept the notion that the works he wrote in different genres may be just as good as the ones that follow the traditional German formal line? The question suggests its own answer: Brahms remained true to his era's definition of aesthetic purity, and he had the right ethnic credentials. Dvořák did not have them and, in any case, felt compelled to succeed on a much broader canvas. Brahms upheld a great tradition; Dvořák created one.

Dvořák was extremely reticent about both his person and his music. The outward circumstances of his life do not lend themselves to simplistic theories about the relationship of individual works to specific biographical events. He had a happy childhood and a supportive family network, entered into a loving marriage with a good woman, and fathered a large family (despite the tragic deaths of several of his young children, as was sadly typical at the time). Thanks to ceaseless hard work and astonishing productivity, Dvořák prospered as both a composer and a teacher, achieving a comfortable degree of financial success as well as international acclaim in his own lifetime. He was unbelievably well traveled: what other great composer of the day journeyed from St. Petersburg to Omaha? This sort of personal history too often erroneously leads to accusations of superficiality and pandering to the popular taste, as though only suffering and misery produce greatness, while shrewd career management, sanity, and cheer inevitably lead to shallowness.

Adding fuel to the fire, Dvořák's work lacks theoretical pretentiousness, and its beguiling melodic exterior continually risks underestimation for the same reason that Mozart's so often does: because it always sounds so recklessly *pretty*. Music that offers such a highly polished surface tends to discourage investigation of its depths, even to the point where some may deny that there are any. Dvořák certainly has the necessary substance, or his output would not enjoy even the selective popularity and respect that it does today. The remainder of this book, then, rests on the assumption—thanks to a bountiful and ever-swelling crop of recordings—that the selective aspect of his popularity rests less on questions of absolute quality than on the unwillingness of some to spend the time required to assimilate the majority of what he wrote, combined with a host of mistaken assumptions.

However, when all is said and done, there truly *is* an amazing story here, not in the uninteresting details of Dvořák's private life, but in the remarkable saga of how a kid from the Bohemian countryside created a personal language of universal appeal and, in so doing, gave an entire nation its musical identity—even jumpstarting the process in at least two others (England and the United States) along the way. What could be a more fascinating subject than this for any music lover? You certainly won't find many other composers whose reach extends as far back as Bach and Handel, and simultaneously as far forward as Art Tatum. Surely it is high time to dismiss the stale judgments of the past as well as the facile assumptions of the present, and instead start listening to both the familiar and unfamiliar works of the romantic era's most versatile genius.

Symphonies and Concertos

The second half of the nineteenth century began as a bad time for the German symphonic tradition. After Beethoven, only Schumann and Mendelssohn carried the torch forward, and neither of those composers was recognized primarily as a symphonist—indeed, they still aren't. Schubert's two most important works in the form (the "Great" and "Unfinished" Symphonies) were either little known (the former) or unplayed (the latter, until 1865, the year of Dvořák's First and Second). Wagner, in a typically self-serving piece of propaganda, declared the symphony to be "dead." He was wrong in the long run, of course, but it's easy to understand his perspective, as he was in part simply offering an explanation for the contemporary situation, evident since Beethoven's day. Even then symphonies were becoming a rarity: Beethoven completed only nine, as compared to Haydn's 107 and Mozart's sixty or so (not to mention the hundreds of other works in the form by lesser composers active during the same period).

The main reasons for this state of affairs were social and economic as well as artistic, beginning with the cultural destruction wrought by the French Revolution and the Napoleonic Wars and culminating, after half a century of political unrest, in the turmoil of 1848. The old system of aristocratic patronage for the musical arts was vanishing, while the rise of the middle classes and the widespread demand for public-performance institutions finally led to the creation of regular orchestral concerts only in the 1840s, and even then on a very limited basis in a few major cities. Orchestras have always been expensive to organize and maintain, and composers, even romantic ones, do not often write music out of inner impulse absent any hope of a scheduled premiere.

This doesn't mean that there weren't plenty of musicians at the time writing symphonies. There certainly were. Nevertheless, the musical stars of the first half of the nineteenth century (aside from opera singers) were not making a living as symphonists but as virtuoso composer/performers, whether violinists like Paganini or pianists like Chopin and Liszt. The focus of serious music-making shifted from the aristocratic residence, with its private orchestra or even opera house, to the bourgeois living room or salon. Chamber music, songs, and piano pieces for domestic consumption comprised the bulk of the new music, with symphonic concerts and operatic productions of high quality limited to the largest and wealthiest national and regional capitals.

The enlargement of the symphony in Beethoven's hands—from a light concert opener or "overture" (as symphonies were called for most of the eighteenth century) to a big, complex feature attraction—also acted as a brake on production. In a very real sense, the form outgrew its traditional purpose and context, and it was only with the general European recovery after 1850 and the rise of civic institutions geared toward promotion of the arts (often from a nationalistic angle) that symphonic production revived. It's surely no accident that in the mid-1860s, three of the four major symphonic composers of the nineteenth century's latter half—Dvořák, Tchaikovsky, and Bruckner—all created their first significant efforts in the genre. Of these three, Dvořák was the first, if only by a hair (see " Dvořák Timeline"), and significantly, both he and Tchaikovsky stood outside the German musical mainstream.

Dvořák was the most successful of these new symphonists in reconciling the genre's classical roots with the romantic love of virtuoso display, heightened emotional expression, integration of ethnic or national musical elements, and colorful exploitation of the full resources of the modern orchestra. Tchaikovsky attempted a similar synthesis, but his achievement has always been more controversial. Bruckner's style was so idiosyncratic that international recognition and acceptance of his achievement remains a late-twentieth-century phenomenon, while Brahms was indeed an end and not a beginning, a glorious summation of the German classical spirit.

Dvořák loved and admired this symphonic tradition. He was no revolutionary, but he possessed both the stylistic individuality and the self-confidence to broaden and deepen its frame of reference just enough to give the medium itself a fresh new look. You might call his symphonies conservative, but with strongly liberal leanings. More than any others of the period, his nine works in the genre successfully walk the fine line between respectful homage and originality of form and content.

Dvořák's Symphonic Style

Symphony No. 1 ("The Bells of Zlonice") (1865)
Symphony No. 2 (1865)
Symphony No. 3 (1872)
Symphony No. 4 (1874)
Symphony No. 5 (1875)
Symphony No. 6 (1880)
Symphony No. 7 (1885)
Symphony No. 8 (1889)
Symphony No. 9 ("From the New World") (1893)

The chart on the opposite page lists the orchestration of each of Dvořák's symphonies and concertos, and at the bottom, I offer the standard instrumentation of the German romantic symphony as often employed by such composers as Mendelssohn and Schumann. Note that none of Dvořák's symphonies follow this paradigm slavishly, nor do any of Brahms's for that matter. The principal sonic distinction between them comes in the handling of the woodwind section (a Czech specialty dating well back into the eighteenth century) and in the use of additional percussion. Whereas Brahms differs from the mean principally at the lower end of the timbral scale, invariably using a tuba or contrabassoon in each of his four symphonies, Dvořák's individuality asserts itself at the upper end, in his preference for the bright and penetrating sounds of piccolo, English horn, and triangle.

By themselves these differences don't amount to much, except for the fact that they highlight a much broader general tendency. The German style of both Brahms and Wagner shares a fondness for deep, dark sounds cushioning a rich middle. Dvořák and his Czech compatriots (including Smetana), in contrast, cultivated a lighter basic sonority with more space between lows and highs. At climaxes, Brahms and Wagner often sound rich and thick, while Dvořák and Smetana tend to sound lean and brash, even strident. This brighter complexion goes hand in hand with Czech music's stronger and more varied rhythmic component—rooted in dance and in the peculiar accentuation of the language—as well as its often pastoral character, typified by particularly colorful exploitation of woodwind timbres.

As the chart suggests, Dvořák's orchestral habits remained consistent in these fundamental qualities throughout his life. They were a legacy of his practical experience in the opera pit and, above all, of the instrumental style of the Italian and French operas that served as the basis of the repertoire that he played. It was there that he discovered his fondness for such instruments

Dvořák Symphonies and Concertos: Orchestration (in addition to strings and timpani)

Symphony	Flute + Piccolo	Oboe + English Horn	Clarinet + Bass Clarinet	Bassoons	Horns	Trumpets	Trombones + Tuba	Percussion	Harp
1	2+1	2+1	2	2	4	2	3		
2	2+1	2	2	2	4	2	3		
3	2+1	2+1	2	2	2	2	3+1	triangle	—
4	2+2	2	2	2	4	2	3	triangle, bass drum, cymbals	—
5	2	2	2+1	2	4	2	3	triangle	
6	2+1	2	2	2	4	2	3+1		
7	2+1	2	2	2	4	2	3		
8	2+1	2+1	2	2	4	2	3+1	triangle, cymbals	
9	2+1	2+1	2	2	4	2	3+1		
Piano Concerto	2	2	2	2	2	2			
Violin Concerto	2	2	2	2	4	2			
Cello Concerto	2+1	2	2	2	3	2	3+1	triangle	
Standard	2	2	2	2	4	2	3		

as the harp, English horn, and bass clarinet. Wagner's particular contribution to this colorful mix, on the other hand, appears almost exclusively in the slow movements of the Third and Fourth Symphonies and hardly anywhere else. It is almost always overstated, both in Dvořák's specific case and within the context of nineteenth-century music generally. Because Wagner's late operas are so highly valued today, he is often viewed in retrospect as a much more influential figure *musically* than he was in his own lifetime, when his writings enjoyed far more currency than the works themselves. The fact that Dvořák liked Wagner's music and participated in a single concert under him in 1863 does not provide a legitimate excuse for ignoring everything else that the young Czech composer played, studied, enjoyed, and found inspirational during his formative years—an issue that I will address in more detail in considering the operas.

Dvořák's synthesis of the various musical options open to him, stylistically speaking, was uniquely personal and present from the beginning. This makes sense if one recalls that Dvořák's "beginning" wasn't especially early. He was no prodigy. The First Symphony—which was written in 1865 for a German composition competition, sent off, and (so Dvořák went to his grave believing) lost forever—is in fact his very first surviving orchestral work of any kind. All the other symphonies were revised carefully prior to performance or publication, and the charge against Dvořák of occasional formal diffuseness stems to some extent from incorrect conclusions drawn in noting this otherwise admirable habit.

When a composer has such a powerful melodic gift, often the only way to judge how best to organize a large work is literally to play it by ear: to listen to it and see how well the tunes sustain the evolving musical structure when heard in context. There's nothing unusual about this. All composers make revisions based on the actual experience of listening, and the only difference in

Dvořák's case is the extent to which he relied on this method and his honesty in admitting it. So the entire controversial issue of his use of form can be reduced to this simple, dogmatic statement: When Dvořák needed to be highly organized, he was, and when he didn't need to be, he wasn't. This doesn't make every work equally strong or appealing, but whether or not you like a given piece probably will not stem primarily from issues relating to Dvořák's handling of form.

Far more interesting and germane to the experience of listening are the numerous melodic archetypes that remain a fixture of Dvořák's work throughout his life and indisputably proclaim his musical originality. In the shape and structure of his tunes, you can hear the sounds that fascinated him and how he bent them to his personal expressive needs: his love of birdsong (he raised pigeons), of the classical tradition, of Czech folk music, of Negro spirituals, of dance rhythms, of marches, and even of locomotives (his other hobby aside from raising pigeons was watching trains). Many of his melodies employ strongly accented repeated notes and evoke the natural rhythms of speech. Others have unusual phrase structures or interesting harmonic twists, or consist of deliberately primitive elements such as simple scales or nursery tunes. Together they comprise Dvořák's musical vocabulary, and all of them are richly represented in his nine symphonies.

Symphony No. 1 ("The Bells of Zlonice")

Zlonice was the town in which Dvořák lived as he was beginning his musical training, although the title of the symphony is only mentioned in a letter written much later in his life, after he thought the score irretrievably lost (it came to light in the 1920s). The bells are graphically represented by the tolling horns of the work's introduction. They return as transitional material during the first-movement exposition, feature prominently in the development, and appear in the triumphant finale as well. This use of what is now called *cyclical form* is unusual for 1865, although Schumann's symphonies apply the principal in a number of imaginative ways, and Dvořák was certainly no stranger to the idea. His very first string quartet (1862) makes use of the principal. Unusual too is the prominence (seldom adequately realized in performance) given the three timpani, which play a five-note rhythmic motto in all four movements. This ubiquitous rhythm first appears in the violins just after the chiming-bell introduction, accompanying the opening theme of the exposition.

There are some oddly impractical features about this score that surely would have been corrected on revision, and which further prevent it from receiving many performances in concert. For example, the English horn only plays a few bars in the first movement (and the part can't be doubled by one of the oboes), which also requires all four horns, whereas the ensuing three movements only ask for a pair. The fact that movements 2 through 4 share the same meter (2/4) risks rhythmic monotony, although a characterful interpretation can largely get around that problem. In virtually all other respects, however, the piece sounds just like Dvořák and remarkably unlike anyone else. Its length has been exaggerated. The whole work (with repeats) runs for about fifty minutes, or as long as Beethoven's "Eroica" Symphony or the first two symphonies of Brahms, when performed with their respective repeats intact. And yet it's considered acceptable to make cuts in this work on those infrequent occasions when it gets played (and recorded).

Consider the opening movement, which has tremendous drive throughout its eighteen minutes. At least eleven minutes are exposition (if repeated), about five minutes are development, and the balance is a highly compressed recapitulation that omits the first theme entirely, reserving it for the coda—exactly as Dvořák would do three decades later in the first movement of the Cello

#1

Concerto, which is universally admired for its formal ingenuity. I'm not claiming that the First Symphony is as great a work as the Cello Concerto (no way!), but it is a fully *characteristic* one as regards both form and content, which in the long run is the more important consideration. Take another example: the shape of this first-movement exposition—which consists of two main subjects, both presented quietly at first, then powerfully in the full orchestra after a short transition—follows essentially the same pattern as that of another acknowledged masterpiece: the opening movement of the Seventh Symphony.

The repeat of an important theme (usually softly, then loudly) prior to moving on, called a *counterstatement* in musical terminology, occurs in all of Dvořák's first-movement expositions to some extent, with the sole exception of that of the Second Symphony. Another constant feature in Dvořák's later work is the omnipresence of little detachable motives (here, that five-note rhythm already mentioned) that serve as connecting tissue, accompaniments, or raw materials for building crescendos and effecting diminuendos, and which propel the music forward with an athletic vigor so characteristic of his music. He has an unlimited store of these rhythmic building blocks. No two are quite the same, but all serve a similar purpose. As with the counterstatement, Dvořák borrowed this technique from Beethoven (the "Eroica" and "Pastoral" Symphonies particularly) but applied it with a versatility and ingenuity that the older composer probably never imagined.

Each of the symphony's four movements displays melodies of a type that will feature prominently in Dvořák's later work. The first subject of the first movement belongs to his store of simple themes that outline the basic harmony. These usually consist of scales or *arpeggios* (broken chords), and in this case the tune consists of little more than a rising and falling scale in the home key of C minor. Themes of this type characterize the first-movement expositions of the Fifth, Seventh, and Ninth Symphonies as well. The lovely slow movement omits the trombones and begins, as do the similar movements of the Third, Sixth, and Seventh Symphonies (as well as the slow movement of the Cello Concerto), with a plaintive woodwind chorale. Its alternation of free variations with marchlike fanfares on the brass characterizes almost all of Dvořák's andantes and adagios, and perhaps was originally inspired by the second movement of Beethoven's Fifth Symphony.

The scurrying scherzo, the only one by Dvořák not in triple time, reveals two particularly prescient features. First is his use of what might be called "functional counterpoint." By this I mean Dvořák's ability to energize his musical textures with bustling independent instrumental lines, without having to write in strict contrapuntal forms such as fugues. He was a master at simultaneously combining themes and also at melodic imitation and overlapping, all accomplished without academic strictness. The witty initial section of this movement provides an ideal case in point. Both its opening and middle sections introduce perhaps Dvořák's most prominent thematic shape, a marchlike tune beginning with three long notes, quite often the same note repeated. You will encounter variants of this idea everywhere in his work, a sort of musical equivalent of the idea: one—two—three—Go! The "Go!" part can be anything at all, from a tiny rhythmic motive to a complete tune, as long as it's preceded by this three-note lead.

The finale opens with another frequently encountered melodic shape, what I will call a "mirror theme." This is a tune made up of two short figures, the second of which is an exact (or almost exact) mirror image of the first. This may sound complicated, but it really isn't. Two famous and familiar examples of such tunes are the opening of Mozart's *Eine Kleine Nachtmusik* and the initial fanfare introducing Haydn's Symphony No. 104 ("London").

You can always tell these kinds of tunes because one phrase goes up, the other down (or vice versa). Despite the fact that Dvořák offsets the somewhat foursquare rhythms of this finale with some arresting harmonic adventures and little jets of color from the piccolo, it's still the weakest movement in the symphony. He knows where he's going but isn't quite sure how to get there. Oddly enough, the music's homespun, at-times-awkward frankness bears a very curious and striking resemblance to the much later first two symphonies of American iconoclast Charles Ives (of all people).

Dvořák's lack of polish here probably stems more from an overabundance of individual character than an absence of sheer technique. When the finale eventually does pull itself together for its final peroration, it reveals another habit of Dvořák's borrowed from Beethoven's Fifth: a love of big, long, brassy codas. None of his symphonies conclude quietly, and all of them (except the Third) follow the standard classical pattern of having the scherzo or dance movement in the third position. This means a steady increase in energy following the first movement, invariably leading to a loud, although not necessarily happy, ending. Another interesting point not often mentioned is that four of Dvořák's symphonies (including this one) begin in dark, turbulent minor keys, and two of them (Nos. 7 and 9) have tragic finales—food for thought to be considered in further detail shortly.

Symphony No. 2

Having shipped off the first symphony to someplace in Germany, we know not where or why, Dvořák immediately sat down and wrote another one. This time, however, he hung onto it, although it was only performed once in his lifetime—in 1888, twenty-three years after its original date of composition—and published as late as 1959. The reasons for the delay have little to do with the quality of the music, which Dvořák thoroughly revised prior to the premiere. Beethoven composed a single "Pastoral" Symphony, but Dvořák wrote three, in mood if not in name, and this is the first of them (the others are Nos. 5 and 8). It is without question the most relaxed and bucolic-sounding large orchestral work in existence after its Beethovenian model. Any problems attendant on listening tend to vanish as soon as one accepts the fact that this is indeed a pastoral work, and so its easy fluency and mellifluousness reflect the composer's deliberate intention, and not his inability to write something of a different character entirely.

Each movement of this symphony begins with an introduction, with a very obvious similarity between the opening of the first and third movements. Otherwise, unlike the First Symphony, this one has no important cyclical features (that is, shared themes or motives). The first movement's introduction, after eight long, velvety notes from the strings against sustained wind chords, offers both the exposition's first theme and a foretaste of the rambunctious transition material between this tune and the second subject. Then the music rapidly calms down in preparation for the beginning of the exposition.

Please don't get the impression from the ensuing description that this movement consists of nothing but rounded edges and fuzzy musical daydreams. Actually, much of the material is extremely lively. The key to Dvořák's strategy resides in the fact that the principal themes (there are three of them) are indeed all gentle and winsome, but at the same time all of the transitional material between them, without exception, is boisterous and rhythmically charged. So the effect he produces is one of continual relaxation after successive bursts of energy. This also accounts for the introduction's use of the vivacious transition theme, permitting Dvořák to ease into the exposition proper, thus setting the tone for the remainder of the movement. Only at the very end do the vigorous elements succeed in displacing the gentler ones, and therein lies much of the music's humor and charm. It increasingly wakes up as it goes, as does the entire symphony.

The second and third themes of this exposition are particularly personal, as they both incorporate that three long-note melodic shape from the First Symphony's third movement. In the second subject, this occurs as the second half of a larger idea, and the three notes are the same; whereas in the third subject, they are each different, but the rhythmic similarity is clear. This third subject will also do double duty as the movement's exciting coda. Prior to that, however, comes an expansive development section rather flagrantly modeled on Beethoven's Sixth, consisting of a leisurely series of repetitive accumulations of small rhythmic figures derived from the principal tunes, with further thematic variants floating above and around them.

The moment of recapitulation is easy to hear. The perpetual undulations of the development stop, and Dvořák returns to the opening theme, unadorned and almost unharmonized, in dialogue between violins and woodwind. It's typical that the approach to the recapitulation, so often a passage of high drama in classical- and romantic-period symphonies alike, here becomes the most starkly tranquil episode in the entire work, memorable for its very simplicity and lack of pretense. It may not raise the roof, but it really is very beautifully and movingly done. A large and vigorous passage of further development then intervenes before the return of the second subject, after which the coda follows quickly, ending the movement in high spirits.

Remarks concerning the profoundly lovely second movement (which retains the full orchestra) range all over the map. Some claim it shares a kinship with the "Scene by the Brook" from Beethoven's "Pastoral" Symphony because it has the same meter (12/8) and a certain flowing movement throughout. Others mention Wagner, God only knows why, for it sounds nothing like him at all. I have another suggestion. In 1864 Smetana and his orchestra (which included Dvořák) performed Berlioz's *Roméo et Juliette*. If you listen to the famous "Scène d'amour" (Love Scene), you will find a remarkable coincidence in mood and texture, as well as in the shape of some of the melodies. There's the same twilit atmosphere, with long-limbed tunes broadly sung by dusky-toned strings (the violins and cellos often together); the same hints of birdsong and nocturnal rustlings in the accompaniments; and those soulful, tender melodies given to the woodwinds. There are also formal similarities, such as the way the introduction, which in both cases is pure mood-setting defining no specific theme, returns after the big opening paragraph before the music moves on to a more agitated central section.

I am not generally a fan of biographical interpretations of purely musical ideas, particularly absent hard evidence (by which I mean the composer himself coming out and saying "This is what it means"), but we do know that Dvořák was at the time seriously in love with one of his students (Josefina by name). In 1865, the same year as this symphony, he composed a cycle of love songs (*Cypresses*) in tribute to her that occupied him for the rest of his life in various versions. No one knows what motivated him to write this symphony, but I am more than willing to throw down the gauntlet in this one specific case and declare this second movement to be both love music and, more particularly, strongly influenced by Berlioz. You can compare the two works yourself and draw your own conclusions.

And speaking of biographical interpretations, the scherzo, which sounds like absolutely no one but Dvořák and has no precedent in any previous music, contains the first of what I call his "train tunes." On first encounter, I casually associated some of Dvořák's melodies with musical depictions of locomotives, so imagine my surprise to discover that he had what amounted to a fetishistic fascination with them. I'm not suggesting that he ever literally attempted to capture a train in music, as for example Honegger's famous symphonic poem *Pacific 231*. Dvořák did, however, write several industrial-strength melodies accompanied by regular, chugging rhythms that convey the impression of rapid, powerful physical movement. So "train tune" is as good a term to characterize them as any, and it has the additional advantage of being true to the biographical facts.

The scherzo opens with a variant of the first-movement introduction, complete with a lively climax that winds down to introduce the gracious principal theme. You may note the presence of the piccolo, which now joins the wind section, trilling merrily on high. The irreverent comments from the woodwinds between the two big statements of the principal melody reveal Dvořák at his most witty. Another big crescendo, abruptly cut off, introduces the train tune, full of bounding rhythms thrust forward by timpani riffs and culminating in a series of brilliant brass fanfares. These in turn summon the ghost of the introduction, which rapidly dissolves into the central (*trio*) section. Rhythmic motives in the winds (similar to those that will open the Fourth Symphony) accompany a wide-spanning tune on horns and cellos that sounds a bit like "I've Been Workin' on the Railroad" (as long as we're on the subject).

Later, a dialogue between strings and woodwinds, like a subconscious recollection of the tiny woodwind codetta from the end of Gilda's "Caro nome" (Verdi's *Rigoletto* had its first performance in 1864 at the Provisional Theater where Dvořák played), leads back to the introduction. A not-quite-complete restatement of the opening section then launches a lengthy coda that gradually winds its way to a peaceful close. Some of the thematic material here also resembles the main tune in Smetana's overture to *The Bartered Bride*, that quintessential Czech masterpiece. The only catch is that Dvořák wrote the symphony first, demonstrating persuasively that to the extent that his music sounds specifically Czech, it was a quality present from the outset and not merely a cloak that he donned in the more specifically nationalist works of the late 1870s.

The piccolo sticks around for the finale, and has some really exciting licks in it later on, but the movement begins with another vintage tune, a breezy and exhilarating gem that only Dvořák could have written. Although nominally in a sort of *sonata form* (that is, having an exposition, a development, and a recapitulation), this finale hangs together simply on the strength of its melodies and requires nothing other than that you enjoy each moment as it comes. The exposition has three parts: the opening theme that quickly reaches a climax in a series of brass fanfares; a long transition introduced by one of Dvořák's childlike nursery tunes, building to yet another set of fanfares; and finally, a positively luscious lyrical theme, thrillingly accompanied by metallic string tremolos played *sul ponticello* (on the bridge of the instrument). Dvořák liked this particular special effect: it also occurs in the finale of the Third Symphony and the first movement of the Sixth, among other places.

As the movement continues, the lyrical theme assumes greater and greater prominence, until it unites triumphantly with brass fanfares and pounding timpani to bring the symphony to a close. Even the last bars have a distinctive jet of color in the form of the rumbling cellos and basses heard between the loud chords on the full orchestra. It's really a scandal that this work isn't better known and performed at least once in a while. Not only does it contain a full helping of beautiful music, but taken along with the First Symphony, it reveals Dvořák at age twenty-four to have had all the makings of the great composer to come—in particular, a musical profile strong and original enough to assimilate a wide range of outside influences and put them to good use without ever sounding merely derivative.

By the way, if you find the thought of checking out two big early Dvořák symphonies intimidating, then try the piano cycle called *Silhouettes*. These little pieces contain many of the best tunes from both works, and you can always go back and compare. I discuss the piano rewrites more fully in chapter 4.

Symphony No. 3

This was the symphony that, in 1875, brought Dvořák to the attention of Brahms for the first time and won him a state stipend for promising composers that relieved him of some of his immediate financial worries. It may sound surprising that a work with marked Wagnerian influences in its slow movement and finale, along with an unusual large-scale formal organization (only three movements), should have garnered the approval of the notoriously conservative composer and his equally conservative friends on the grant committee. In fact, this is the symphony in which Dvořák begins the self-willed process of returning to his classical roots, structurally speaking, to such a degree that it would have been difficult for Brahms not to have seen it.

Specifically, the first movement is one of the very few examples in the entire romantic period of monothematic sonata form of the kind that Haydn practiced with particular enthusiasm. Only the orchestration—which includes tuba and English horn in the first two movements, a harp in the second, and a piccolo and triangle in the third—could be said to reflect more modern tendencies. The combination of richly romantic orchestration, arresting thematic material, and tight construction (for example, no exposition repeat in the first movement) speaks for itself. If any of Dvořák's early symphonies deserves to become a repertory item, it is this one. There's no other work of the period quite like it.

I have included the entire first movement on CD 1, track 1. It's not terribly long: only about ten minutes, as befits a sonata movement founded on only a single principle tune—one of the most beautiful ever to open a symphony. Not only is it lovely when taken as a whole, but Dvořák fills it with figures that permit it to be developed and extended as the music proceeds. In other words, it's not merely pretty; it's smart too. The movement opens with a few bars of rhythmic introduction, after which that glorious tune sails in on violins and woodwinds. The English horn makes its plaintive tone felt right from the beginning, at 0:54. This partial repetition of the theme breaks off and leads to a big climax culminating in a counterstatement (that is, a full repeat of the theme) at 1:43, exultantly arranged for the entire orchestra. Growing in intensity as it turns the last gesture of the tune into an independent rhythmic motive (at 2:02), the climax comes to an abrupt halt, and with a few quizzical gestures, the second subject sails in graciously, on the violins.

This theoretically new idea, first heard at 2:36, should sound familiar, as it's merely an expansion of the opening theme's second phrase, a four-note descending motive. Compare this to the music at 0:13, and you'll hear the derivation immediately. Note that the little melodic "turn" from the tune's first phrase now accompanies this new idea, yielding yet another detachable independent motive. The only other important idea in the movement is the energetic transition theme, which you have already heard more than once. It first shows up immediately after the first presentation of the main melody, at 0:39, and like the second subject, it derives directly from it, only in this case it's simply a fragment of the melodic turn from the first phrase, repeated and expanded several times.

The development section starts at 4:00 with a minor-key version of the opening tune, but the second subject interrupts immediately and takes over, except for a brief appearance by the transition theme at 5:24. A violent climax beginning with four repetitions of the second subject (5:39 to 6:13) leads to the recapitulation and the return of the main theme at 7:36. Because Dvořák spent most of the development working with the second subject, he omits it entirely for the remainder of the movement (it's automatically included in the first subject, in any case). This very effective technique of "short circuiting" is not unusual for him: he did it in the first movement of the First Symphony, and he will do it again, famously, in the Cello Concerto. The balance of the movement, then, consists of an expansive coda that includes a good bit of further development of the main theme, as it was largely absent from the development section, before concluding in triumph.

Increasing density of thought often goes hand in hand with a wider emotional range. The opening of the large central movement, a funeral march in all but name, contains some of the darkest music in any Dvořák symphony. Its form is simple: ABA–coda (B). The first A section consists of a broad series of laments featuring English horn, cellos, and rhythmic interjections from the timpani. When these sad strains have run their course, the consoling B section begins with a solemn Wagnerian chorale for brass with harp. It also has a middle section: a thrilling, noble, totally un-Wagnerian tune backed by throbbing wind chords. Dvořák reused it in his *Legend No. 6* (CD 2, track 8, at 2:08). The chorale returns even more grandly, doing its best to sound like the wedding march from *Lohengrin*, accompanied by the festive violins of the *Tannhäuser* overture. A sudden pause leads to a shortened reprise of the A section, with a brief return of B providing a coda of transfigured calm.

The finale also has a simple, very compact, and original structure in two halves: first a simple ABC, then, for the second half, A–development–B–development–C–coda. Timpani touch off a short, theme-free introduction that has no other purpose than to present the movement's omnipresent dotted rhythm. Theme A, in that same rhythm, begins with the perky entry of the triangle and leads immediately through a loud climax to B, a wittily brief gloss on the "big tune" from the allegro section of the *Tannhäuser* overture. Wagner disciples who assume that everyone influenced by the Master invariably borrows in a spirit of reverent homage would be horrified by the amused assurance in evidence here.

A long passage of transition follows, once again in dotted rhythms. As for C, well, it's a cheeky mirror tune (four notes down, then up), also in dotted rhythm, with a prominent piccolo that all but begs for a laugh from the audience. The second development section gets everyone into a hilarious rhythmic mess before C returns one last nose-thumbing time, initiating an exhilaratingly comic conclusion. It's all over in about eight minutes. A more prizeworthy symphony it would be hard to imagine.

Symphony No. 4

Another unjustly neglected work, the Fourth Symphony continues the process already mentioned in connection with the Third Symphony of achieving greater concision and formal strictness while exploring some of the more colorful possibilities of the romantic orchestra. All four movements are exceptionally clear in structure, boldly articulated, and easy to follow. The music's classical spirit finds a corresponding outlet in its tragicomic emotional ambience, and this has been the greatest stumbling block to a wider appreciation of its many virtues. After all, the key of D minor is that of Beethoven's Ninth, and the very opening of the first movement pays homage to that great symphony's cosmic initial measures, as mysterious orchestral stirrings and rhythmic fragments gradually build to a jagged, fanfarelike theme in the full orchestra—only to yield with shocking immediacy to the graceful waltz that comprises the second subject.

Romantic symphonies in minor keys aren't supposed to give up on them so quickly. Classical symphonies, on the other hand (Haydn's especially), do it all the time, using the minor tonality more as a kind of musical spice or flavoring than as an invitation to grand outpourings of pain. It's interesting to compare this work to Haydn's Symphony No. 80 (also in D minor), another brilliant exercise in tragicomedy that has never quite been forgiven as a result. There is in this symphony a certain self-deprecating refusal to take itself terribly seriously that I find peculiarly Czech, and I cannot believe that Dvořák did not understand the implications of writing in particularly well-organized traditional forms, but with an expressive playfulness largely foreign to the German romantic school. I think it's worth giving him credit, as a man past thirty and a practicing musician of enormous experience, for knowing exactly what he was doing here.

So as noted, the half-stern, half-lyrical opening movement treats three basic ideas: the rhythmic fragments on the woodwinds ①
from the mysterious introduction, the big minor-key eruption for ②
full orchestra to which they lead, and the gracious waltz tune ③
that comprises the second subject. There's very little padding. Transitions are short, even abrupt, and this highlights the music's almost manic mood shifts, while at the same time making the form schematically clear. The development section pits the introduction's rhythmic fragments against the waltz, both separately and in combination, leading to a very well-timed and exciting return to the first subject for full orchestra. Because this tune was entirely absent from the previous development, Dvořák spends some time with it now (compare the similar case in the Third Symphony's first movement). When the waltz finally returns, it has lost much of its ebullience, and so it yields

to the darkness of the introduction, with the big D-minor theme actually having the last word.

The second movement is a theme and variations, a form at which Dvořák was one of music's supreme masters. Scored for clarinets, bassoons, horns, and trombones in his best imitation of the opening of Wagner's *Tannhäuser* overture, the actual tune, with its three long, descending notes at the beginning, is pure Dvořák and rather better than its model. One of the more interesting things about musical imitations is that they often improve on the originals. I always get the strong impression that whenever Dvořák copies Wagner (or anyone else), it's never with an intent to hide the resemblance, but rather to make a point of it, as if to say: "Isn't this nifty? See, I can do it too."

Those first three notes detach themselves and become the subject of the movement's single stormy episode, while the harp, sensitively used, adds a gentle wash of color from time to time. The variations are quite easy to follow, mostly retaining the shape of the original melody. Although a very beautiful and perfectly serious piece of writing in its own right, the irony of using Wagner, the guy who declared the symphony "dead," as the inspiration for a set of classical-style variations could not have escaped Dvořák, or Brahms for that matter. This was another of the works that earned Dvořák state financial support and led to his friendship with the elder composer.

As happened in the Second Symphony, the scherzo begins with a variation of the first movement's introduction, leading in this case to the greatest of all Dvořák's train tunes: a surging, chugging melody on woodwinds and horns, accompanied its second time around by swirling violins and harp. It's unforgettably vivid. The central trio section is a plebian march scored with Mahlerian brashness: the two flutes switch to piccolos, and Dvořák adds bass drum, cymbals, and triangle, crashing away with vulgar enthusiasm. In today's multicultural world, with its more tolerant attitude toward such examples of musical eclecticism, it's possible to enjoy this music without feeling guilty or worrying about tired conventional assumptions as to what constitutes "good taste." There's also a very respectable precedent (and possible inspiration) for this music: the unapologetically folksy trio of the scherzo of Beethoven's Seventh Symphony. The march cuts off abruptly, and a short transition brings back the scherzo proper, but instead of the loud repetition of the train tune, it leads to a surprising return of the march, this time minus percussion, and a still more unexpected minor-key close.

The compact finale intensifies the dichotomy already revealed in the first movement: its principal, minor-key theme is even more rhythmically stiff than previously, while the lyrical second subject is even more freely rhapsodic. That first theme is for many the most problematic idea in the entire symphony. It's a sort of ur-Dvořákian primal motive made up of five-note phrases in mirror form (first going up, then down), with the first three notes repeated. As a subject for symphonic development, it's pretty much hopeless, but the theme evidently doesn't understand this, so the development section is in fact one of the most exciting that Dvořák ever wrote. All joking aside, this clunky tune exists for three purposes: to provide maximum contrast with the lyrical second subject, to combine with it rhythmically (on the timpani) at the movement's climax, and to be funny in the mock-pompous coda. It accomplishes all these objectives in about ten minutes with consummate ease.

There's one more interesting fact about this finale. It is the very first example in a romantic symphony of what would become almost a cliché in the hands of later composers: the return of the lyrical "big tune" by way of providing the movement's natural climax at the end. Both Tchaikovsky (First Piano Concerto) and Rachmaninov (Piano Concertos Nos. 2 and 3; Symphony No. 2) found this technique much to their liking, although they could not have known Dvořák's use of it here. It may be that the whole trend started with the Grieg Piano Concerto (1868), but whatever the ultimate source, this is the only time that Dvořák created a finale of this particular type. Once its basically humorous character is accepted at face value, it turns out to be good fun and, more importantly, all of a piece with the rest of the work.

Symphony No. 5

The second of Dvořák's three pastoral symphonies, the Fifth's bucolic instrumental colors (favoring the woodwind section) and rustic melodies proclaim a kinship to the great classical tradition of "outdoors" music. It would be wrong, though, to consider the piece in any way dull, lacking in energy, or bland in terms of expressive intensity. Dvořák in pastoral mode is primarily lively, and this symphony spends as much time in and around the darker minor keys as does the Fourth, nominally in D minor. Although this work does in fact share the same key (F major) as Beethoven's famous "Pastoral" Symphony, it owes much less to it than does Dvořák's Second.

Generally considered to be the first of his "great" symphonies, the differences in technical mastery between it and its predecessors are in fact rather slight. Remember that the classical approach to form does not mean following pre-established rules, but rather rising to the challenge of finding the structure that best reveals the expressive depth of the material at hand. It's surely no accident that this work impressed Brahms, perhaps to the degree (as I mentioned in chapter 1) that it had a demonstrative influence on his own Third Symphony, also in F major and notably bucolic in character. The fact that most commentators acknowledge this particular symphony's excellence has not, alas, made it any more likely to be heard in concert than any of Dvořák's earlier, theoretically less deserving works.

The symphony's opening practically defines the word *pastoral*, with clarinets, then flutes, playing one of Dvořák's simple arpeggio themes. This introduction leads to a racy new tune for full orchestra with prominent horns. Note that the design of this passage exactly resembles that of the beginning of the Fourth Symphony, but the melodies and moods are entirely different. The same holds true for the second subject, which, although not in waltz-rhythm as in the Fourth Symphony, is otherwise an almost identical tune consisting of three rising and falling phrases. This ultimately alternates with loud outbursts, until a stern, minor-key summons from the horns followed by trombones brings the exposition to a close. These four basic elements are so distinctive in and of themselves, and the progress of the music so effortless, that the development and recapitulation require no further comment.

The andante and scherzo that follow belong together. Dvořák explains this to his listeners by composing a linking passage that covers the harmonic distance between them, but more than that, these two movements are to some extent mirror images of each other. Both are in 3/8 time, but the andante is slow while the scherzo, nominally a Czech dance called a *furiant*, is quick. Both have the same simple form: ABA. The A section of the andante begins in a soulful minor key on the cellos, veers toward brighter major keys, then concludes back in the minor. The A section of the scherzo begins in the major in the woodwinds (later joined by the triangle), veers toward darker minor keys, then concludes back in the major. Finally, the main theme of the B section of the scherzo is nothing more than a modest variation of the one in the andante. However fascinating these observations regarding form may be, they can't begin to describe the sheer melodic charm and harmonic richness of both movements.

Dvořák launches the finale at full throttle, with a grinding minor-key theme in cellos and basses. This gets repeated, rescored, and discussed on the way to a brilliant climax that passes smoothly into a svelte second subject in dialogue between woodwinds and violins. The exposition concludes with an ethereal woodwind chorale accompanied by murmuring strings. Suddenly, the horns blast out the second subject, trumpets announce the opening theme, and the development begins dramatically. The woodwind chorale intervenes once more, only to be interrupted by the horns as before, only from a different harmonic angle. An even more furious discussion ensues, finally collapsing in the exhausted tones of the solo bass clarinet (its only appearance in the symphony).

The recapitulation features a ghostly reprise of the opening theme but otherwise reviews all the tunes in their original order, only this time the ethereal chorale passes imperceptibly into the harmonies of the symphony's opening theme. This wakes up the rest of the orchestra, and an amazingly vigorous coda breezes in. At the very end, the trumpets turn the finale's opening theme into a fanfare, while the trombones simultaneously blast out the clarinet tune from the beginning of the first movement. Thus united, trumpets lead the charge to the brilliantly jubilant final bars. Dvořák has at last achieved that elusive, perfect balance between originality of expression and respect for the great classical tradition. He has another quarter century of creative life ahead of him, and there will be no looking back.

Symphony No. 6

This symphony gets trotted out now and again by enterprising conductors, with both audiences and critics often expressing surprise that such a masterpiece remains so infrequently heard, especially compared to the hopelessly overexposed piece that theoretically inspired it: the Second Symphony of Brahms. As

I noted in the chapter 1, the two works actually have little in common, the Brahms being his most mellow and lyrical work in the genre, while the Dvořák is more heroic in tone, more rhythmically lively, and believe it or not, a bit more compact in structure. I am not saying that this symphony is "better" than Brahms's, merely that the differences are much greater than the superficial similarities and that there's nothing particularly useful to be gained by making the comparison in the first place.

The symphony opens with a gently syncopated rhythm in the horns and violas, over which woodwinds and lower strings take turns with a typical Dvořák thematic archetype: the "question and answer" melody. One section responds to the other in alternation, and they come together at the tune's climax. A busy bit of string writing leads to a fortissimo counterstatement of this main theme, now for the violins answered by the full brass section, reaching a brilliant climax that once again reveals Dvořák's ability to be grandiose without a hint of bombast. The melody subsides into a chugging train tune for the strings, breaking off suddenly to a quizzical strain from the violins. Flutes begin the transition to the second subject in gentle imitation of the rugged theme in the identical place in Beethoven's *Egmont* overture.

When it finally arrives, the second subject turns out to be a perky but lyrical oboe melody, which, like the first theme, bursts out in the full orchestra in a glorious counterstatement, sung by violins with caroling horns adding a joyous counterpoint. This exposition may or may not be repeated (as is the case with all the symphonies offering that option), but in 1891 Dvořák left written instruction canceling the repeat "once and for all," so Czech performances never make it, despite the fact that the lead-back is quite beautiful. The development section consists entirely of variations on the opening theme and its transitional material (note especially the lovely moment where the *Egmont* tune appears in the flutes atop those metallic *sul ponticello* string tremolos first heard in the Second Symphony's finale). Accordingly, the recapitulation omits the grand counterstatement of the first theme but includes the full second subject, leading immediately to a busy coda that combines several of the main themes in joyful counterpoint on the way to its brass-laden climax.

As with most of Dvořák's slow movements, this one is a sort of theme and variations, but it comes across almost like one continuous melody that returns to its opening measures every so often, only to be interrupted by a single stormy outburst towards the end. The woodwinds provide a plaintive introduction to the theme, heard on the violins, but there's really no obvious way to analyze or describe it, other than to note that the main tune begins with three long notes (not the same), as so many of Dvořák's melodies do. These three notes seem to take on a life of their own, turning into any number of accessory themes as the music progresses (they serve as the basis for the turbulent interlude just mentioned, as happens also in the slow movement of the Fourth Symphony). Both the introduction and the conclusion of the movement seem to pay a passing homage to the great adagio from Beethoven's Ninth Symphony.

The rhythmically dazzling scherzo is one of Dvořák's most formally traditional: AABBCCD–D varied–AB (with C and D representing the central trio section). Its originality lies in the fact that what inhabits this severely traditional form is no standard minuet or scherzo but a Czech furiant, very different from the one in the Fifth Symphony and quite close in tone to the famous Slavonic Dances. The trio section features exquisitely delicate exchanges between strings and woodwinds, with each phrase capped by serene bird calls from the solo piccolo. Both here and in the slow movement (as also in the Fifth and Eighth Symphonies), the trombones take a break, adding an additional lightness and transparency to the orchestration. You can hear this particularly appealing movement on CD 1, track 2. I offer a little key to where each section begins (it obviously opens with A):

B: 0:30
C: 3:20 (the trio's first half)
D: 5:05 (the trio's second half, an even lovelier pastoral interlude)
D-varied: 5:58

The finale opens with a lovely theme played at low volume and with seeming leisure by the full string section. The energy rapidly increases as the rest of the orchestra joins in, leading to a full counterstatement that has the physical energy of one of Dvořák's train tunes. This melody literally skids to a halt to make way for the second subject, a simple sort of nursery theme that ends with a three-note figure similar to the one that opened the slow movement. Another very simple melody, this one beginning with three repeated notes, leads to a cadence theme on horns and woodwinds. The development section makes great play (as did the slow movement) with the second subject's detachable three-note figure, appearing in innumerable combinations alongside the first subject. It builds to a huge climax with pounding timpani and imposing brass belting out the opening theme, leading in decrescendo to the recapitulation.

A final review of all the main themes in their original order initiates a brilliant coda, which, like that of the first movement, begins with a passage of exciting counterpoint in the strings. Over this busy texture, the woodwinds and horns break up the main theme into little two-note fragments, until the brass blast in with heroic fanfares, and the entire orchestra barrels its way to the finish line with one last, grand chorale based on the movement's opening theme. This was the symphony that most helped to make Dvořák's reputation abroad, particularly in England, the country that proved most receptive to his music apart from his homeland and for which he wrote so many superb pieces (choral works especially). If your local orchestra happens to program it, I strongly recommend that you grab a ticket and go.

Symphony No. 7

If the Fifth is the first "great" Dvořák symphony, then the Seventh is widely regarded as the first "astronomically great" Dvořák symphony: indeed, for many it's the greatest of all, although this usually is code for "most like Brahms." It is, in truth, Dvořák's ultimate formal homage to the classical style: a deliberate attempt to appeal to a public and press trained to revere it above all else. At the same time, the music speaks in Dvořák's own personal voice as eloquently and with as much melodic generosity as ever. It's also a grandly tragic symphony, his first of two. If you have time, comparison with Brahms's Fourth Symphony is particularly interesting, as both were written virtually simultaneously (Dvořák's about half a year earlier) and share certain formal as well as emotional characteristics, such as first movements without exposition repeats and those angry, tragic finales.

The most remarkable thing about the Seventh, formally, is its compactness. It plays for about thirty-five minutes on average, making it his shortest symphony but one (the Third), comparable to Brahms's Third, which impressed Dvořák tremendously, as is evident in comparing the opening sounds of Brahms's finale to the first movement of the Dvořák. Indeed, you might say that this symphony picks up where Brahms leaves off, taking on the tragic implications of that last movement and realizing them in an opening of unprecedented cogency and power. The first subject is barely more than the melodic outline of a minor third. Dvořák said that this theme came to him in 1884 on seeing the arrival in the railroad station of a train from Pest. Its continuation (as in the Sixth Symphony) introduces an important new motive: three rising notes of equal length. Both this first theme and the lyrical second subject announced in the clarinets receive full, *fortissimo* counterstatements.

When listening to this movement, pay special attention to what happens in the recapitulation. Dvořák omits the initial soft statement of the opening theme, proceeding directly to its imposing counterstatement. This makes the actual moment of recapitulation the energetic climax of the development and an event of high drama, something that the symphony's quiet opening does not automatically anticipate. But there are greater things to come. Instead of the bright counterstatement of the second subject in its cheerful major key, Dvořák returns to the minor (as Mozart so often does in his minor-key works) and builds a huge climax on the rising three-note transition theme capped by the return of the first subject blasted out on the horns in the form of a fanfare, before the entire movement sinks back into the darkness in which it began.

The slow movement has always been regarded as sublime by just about everyone who talks about it, and yet it contains many of the same elements found way back in the second movement of the First Symphony: the opening on woodwinds; the flowing, improvisatory melodies that seem to play themselves; and a series of climaxes featuring martial music for brass and timpani. The difference lies in how well it all hangs together, the organic sense of flow, and the total lack of padding. Still, however great this music undoubtedly is, the distance traveled in the intervening two decades is not quite as far might be imagined. Do pay special attention, though, to the passage (heard twice) of harmonically mysterious calm, introduced by wandering violins and backed by solemn trombone chords: it's one of music's most profound moments.

Dvořák fans reserve a special place in their hearts for this scherzo, with its pair of initial themes on upper and lower strings presented simultaneously, but in such distinct rhythms that the ear has no trouble sorting them out. The music has a soulful, melancholy grace, unique in the romantic era and equaled only by Mozart in such works as the opening movement of his great G Minor Symphony (No. 40). The trio section, full of birdsong and pastoral woodwind writing, is another of those seemingly endless improvised melodies of which Dvořák alone held the secret. The transition back to the scherzo's main section is impressively dramatic, as are those impassioned decrescendos in the coda, in which the dance gives way to sadness and yearning. You may notice that the scherzo's main theme (initially on the violins), also dwelling largely on the narrow interval of a minor third, is actually a free variation of the first movement's opening.

The finale, which you can hear on CD 1, track 3, opens with a hesitant theme in two parts: a three-note cry of despair from the horns (recognizable as the tune "Bali Ha'i" from the musical *South Pacific*) and a solemn continuation on the strings in march rhythm (at 0:13). There's good reason for the initial hesitation. Dvořák refuses to turn the music loose until the transition (1:26) that leads to the cheerier second subject (2:13), immediately following the first idea's *fortissimo* counterstatement (0:57). As in the first movement, this more lyrical tune also receives a grand counterstatement and an even more energetic cadence theme (2:51). The development section (beginning at 3:20) is mostly quiet and based on sinister, slithery woodwind reiterations of the first subject until, unable to suppress its latent fury any longer, it launches the recapitulation (5:51) with such violence that Dvořák omits the transition theme entirely and moves straight on to the second subject (6:37) in an attempt to reintroduce its happier emotional state.

But the damage has been done: the coda (7:54) makes several attempts to reach an emphatic ending, each try increasing in energy and drive, until grinding harmonies introduce a huge chorale for the full orchestra (8:43) that wrenches the tonality into the major once and for all, ending majestically as if in fulfillment of some preordained destiny. It's a thrilling conclusion to a work that surely deserves the respect it has earned, although it seems a shame that so many exalt this symphony in order to damn with faint praise the two more popular ones that followed. Nor, as you will shortly see, are classical forms, important and satisfying as they are in the hands of a master, the be-all and end-all of symphonic construction and the only valid channels for musical expression.

Symphony No. 8

This is Dvořák's most original symphony, the one most personal in both form and content, and the last of his three "pastoral" symphonies. It's so enjoyable that it is also one of his most-often-performed works, but so unusual in design that I have never seen anyone in the popular literature even attempt to describe its special features accurately. It's as if Dvořák had said, "Okay, I did one Brahms's way, and now I'm going to do it *my* way." Again, the point here is not that one method may be better than the other, but rather that Dvořák's genius was not shackled by the strictures of the classical tradition, much as he revered it. In his last two symphonies, he pushed the boundaries of what a symphony could be a bit further, to the delight of music lovers and the frustration of critics and academics to this very day.

Understanding the form of the first movement is very easy if the description of it focuses on what it actually does, rather than on what standard symphonic first movements are supposed to do. It has three parts (this symphony offers the apotheosis of Dvořák's lifelong obsession with the number three), each part beginning with the same melody. This melody, announced at the start on the cellos, clarinets, bassoons, and horns, backed by soft trombones, has three phrases separated by short pauses. The first two phrases are critically important. Phrase 1 consists of three rising and falling motives of six, seven, and four notes respectively. Pay special attention to the rhythm of its first four notes: long–short–short–long. Phrase 2 consists of two chains of five repeated notes (with a couple of extra notes at the end of each chain), the first of which also contains the rhythm just mentioned.

The third phrase brings the melody to a full stop, and against a shimmering string chord, the flute announces a bird-call theme, beginning with a rising three-note arpeggio, followed by a short continuation in *dotted rhythm* (dum, dadum, dadum, etc.), and ending after a pause with a seven-note tag. This last bit contains (after its first note) a descending three-note arpeggio and a three-note rising figure, again in dotted rhythm. If this sounds confusing, don't worry: when you hear the music, it's as plain as day. Just as important as the theme itself is the fact that Dvořák gives it to the flute, which not only has important solos throughout the symphony, but which also leads the entire woodwind section. More than any other single instrument, the sweet, light, and carefree timbre of the flute characterizes the whole work.

I am describing this material in such detail because every single important tune in the entire symphony is a variation of some bit of this opening. The finale itself is a theme and variations, but so is the entire symphony when you get right down to it. Dvořák had few peers in the art of variation, particularly the melodic variety, where old tunes generate new ones as part of an organic and ongoing process. This, then, was the challenge that he set for himself: to create a big four-movement symphony using a wholly original process of simple melodic variation throughout. How does he do it?

♯8

After the bird-call theme, the orchestra makes a crescendo, ultimately brought up short by the timpani. A new theme immediately follows on violas and cellos. It is, in fact, a variation, consisting of the descending three notes of the bird call's second phrase followed by a five repeated-note chain from the opening theme. On top of this, the flutes continue with the bird call, and it all culminates in a bold counterstatement of that theme for full orchestra, with the violins left to toss out the seven-note tag into mid-air. Woodwinds echo its last three notes in dotted rhythm and introduce a brief transition on the strings. This in turn leads to the second subject, only here it's a variation on that seven-note tag. It begins with the three-note rising figure in dotted rhythm (played three times) in a minor key. A cadence theme brings this entire first section to a close with festive descending scales, the brass capping the whole process with a fanfare consisting of the first three notes (the rising arpeggio) of the bird-call theme with a five repeated-note chain attached, echoed by muted trumpets.

The symphony now starts afresh, from the beginning, except that after the bird-call theme, the mood darkens, and Dvořák begins a vigorous development of that tune, not forgetting to include the viola and cello motive with the five repeated-note chain. Its first three, descending notes detach themselves and become an independent idea. In one particularly memorable episode, this appears menacingly on the lower brass against the bird-call theme in the strings, initiating what can best be called a musical panic attack, as yelping horns launch the recapitulation with a variation of the opening theme, this time blasted out by trumpets atop wailing strings. Having spent most of its time in the development section, the entire bird-call thematic complex now gets reduced to a few bars, mostly on solo English horn (its only appearance in the symphony), and Dvořák instead cuts directly to the second subject, and so on to the cadence tune and a coda based on the bird-call theme's dotted rhythm: da*dum!*

The next two movements of the symphony are both based on the first phrase of the opening theme, and this is easy to hear if you keep in mind its two principal elements: three rising and falling phrases, and the rhythm long–short–short–long. As noted in discussing the previous symphonies, many of Dvořák's slow movements also employ variation form, this one perhaps most wonderfully of them all. You can hear it on CD 1, track 4. The opening theme of this adagio has two parts:

Part 1: Three identical rising and falling phrases arranged in descending sequence. Note the characteristic rhythm, long–short–short–long, after each initial three-note group.

Part 2 (at 0:25): Four quietly muttered repetitions of a four-note motive similar in rhythm to the famous opening of Beethoven's Fifth Symphony: da-da-da-dum.

And here is how Dvořák varies these ideas throughout the movement:

Variation 1 (0:38): Part 1 of the theme takes the shape of a question-and-answer tune: its three-note upbeat becomes a bird call in the flutes (shades of the first movement), answered by a variant from the clarinets of its rising and falling phrase.

Variation 2 (2:05): This is variation 1 played more loudly and in reverse: answer first, then question. Winds, introduced by a roll on the timpani, have the rising and falling phrase, while strings follow with strong statements of the bird call.

Variation 3 (3:00): Part 2 of the theme now becomes a lovely, lyrical tune in the woodwinds incorporating the four-note "Beethoven" motive, atop descending scales in the strings. Notice how the lead-in to this section, on cellos and basses, tells you what part of the tune Dvořák is working with.

Variation 4 (4:01): The descending scales of variation 3 lead to a big climax and fanfare in the brass on the rhythm long–short–

short–long. The melody is the opening phrase of the theme's first part.

Variation 5 (5:22): A reprise of variation 1, with a dark transition in lower strings that leads to:

Variation 6 (6:32): Threatening repetitions of part 1 of the theme in strings and horns eventually gather energy and turn into a typical Dvořák train tune, with chugging rhythms and sharp, regular timpani beats.

Variation 7 (7:21): Slashing string chords interrupt chattering woodwinds and trumpets, together comprising the four-note motives of part 2 of the theme.

Variation 8 (7:51): A reprise of variation 3, rescored for full orchestra. The violins have the tune formerly given to the woodwinds, which now play the descending scales previously heard in the strings.

Variation 9: Coda (9:09): A last variation of the entire theme—with part 1 warmly in the strings, then part 2 in sharp dialogue between strings and winds—leads to a climax in which the bird call of variation 1, high on the violins, separates short five-note trumpet fanfares, including the long–short–short–long rhythm.

The opening phrase of the scherzo—with its three rhythmically identical, wavelike descending sequences sung by the violins—is clearly derived from the string melody at the start of the preceding movement. It is one of the most elegant symphonic waltzes in the entire literature, and the waltz-tune itself has a structure making it a tiny set of progressive variations, in which each succeeding phrase evolves naturally from the preceding one. The waltz has two parts, each consisting of the same opening theme (given to the woodwinds and enriched with a violin countermelody in the second part), which is then followed by three simple variants. The trio section introduces a contrasting idea derived principally from the first phrase of the first movement's opening melody, and also perhaps from variation 3 of the adagio. Note the persistent rhythm: long–short–short–long. The waltz returns unaltered, but the coda is another variation, this time of the entire trio section, delightfully speeded up and leading to a deliciously witty, quiet close.

The finale, the only movement that Dvořák actually calls a "theme and variations," begins with a trumpet fanfare also based on the first phrase of the symphony's initial theme, its characteristic long–short–short–long rhythm leading off. However, the actual principal subject of the variations (on the cellos) is a melody that has two halves, each containing distinct elements heard previously. Its first half clearly comes from the opening movement's bird-call theme and begins with its three-note rising arpeggio. The second half, on the other hand, is a variation on the same idea heard at the start of the following two movements: three rising and falling phrases, only here in ascending rather than descending sequence. So this theme acts as a sort of summary of the content of the entire symphony.

After one simple variation in imitation between lower and upper strings, the movement really takes off. First the theme becomes a very Slavic-sounding scherzo and trio in ABA form. Section A features cheerfully vulgar horn trills and displays in turn the theme's rising three-note opening, the leadoff trumpet fanfare, and the descending phrase in dotted rhythm from the end of the first variation. B, however, is a brilliant flute solo in two halves, both repeated, with a touch of trumpet fanfare on top. The next variation is a march in two parts (the melody beginning with three repeated notes), each reflecting its respective section of the theme. Its second part, also on flute, is particularly interesting because it becomes a tune found elsewhere in Dvořák, most notably in the development section of the first movement of the Piano Trio No. 3 in F Minor. This entire variation gets restated fortissimo and leads to a brief development section, climaxing in the triumphant return of the opening trumpet fanfare.

After all this excitement, the movement settles down to a final group of leisurely, dreamy, very romantic-sounding variations that seemingly have no intention of going anywhere or doing anything. The theme—progressively simplified, ever lazier—ultimately boils down to a series of woodwind repetitions of the rising three-note arpeggio. Suddenly, a reprise of the scherzolike variation erupts out of nowhere and initiates a coda that offers an amazing imitation of a record speeding up from 33 to 78 rpm, only of course records hadn't been invented in 1889. Still, it's a remarkably similar sound. In this carnival atmosphere, the symphony slams to a close with the same da*dum* on the timpani (almost never prominent enough in performance) that concluded the opening movement. It's a shocking, hilariously abrupt conclusion to an extraordinary piece of work that absolutely no one else would have dared write. Haydn would have understood the value of placing such a refined and polished technique in the service of a giant musical joke.

Indeed, the Eighth Symphony's rustic high spirits combine melodic directness and listener appeal with the most subtle formal craftsmanship in a way that truly results in an "art that conceals art." As with all of Dvořák's best music, the tuneful surface is so attractive on its own that it tends to obliterate all other considerations. Still, I think there's value in pointing out that a work sometimes characterized as a mere collection of catchy tunes arranged in a ramshackle musical superstructure stands among the most closely knit pieces of music that Dvořák ever wrote, and that its seemingly endless variety arises from just a few incredibly simple ideas—a rhythm, a phrase-shape, the number three, and a bird-call motive—all of which are present in the symphony's opening minute.

Symphony No. 9 ("From the New World")

For the record, you can call it "From the New World" or, as Dvořák himself often did, just the "New World" Symphony. Like the Eighth, this work has always been very popular, incredibly so. It represents Dvořák's uncanny ability to both judge his audience accurately and continue the line of symphonic development that he had been pursuing all along on his own. There is no conflict of interest between these two goals. On accepting the job as director of the National Conservatory in New York from 1893 to 1895, he knew that he was supposed to write a new work reflecting his impressions of America. That's exactly what he did, but he was smart enough to make sure that the symphony works perfectly well whether or not you look at it from this perspective.

When Dvořák arrived in New York, he gave a newspaper interview in which he expressed his conviction that any national school of American music could only be founded on Negro and American Indian thematic material. This opinion caused a furor on both sides of the Atlantic. While Dvořák's impact on the evolution of American music (especially jazz) has only recently begun to be assessed, there can be little doubt that in conferring aesthetic legitimacy on what he believed to be America's indigenous music, the effect of his backing was huge. Of the 600 students at the National Conservatory, fully one quarter were African American, and his students, both black and white, went on to teach such iconic American figures as George Gershwin, Aaron Copland, and Duke Ellington.

As a member of a minority community himself, born of peasant stock, Dvořák was more than sympathetic to the plight of the former slaves and proud to promote their musical ambitions. What horrified the establishment of the day, though, were not so much his purely artistic claims as the underlying assumption that Native American chants, African American plantation tunes, and spirituals constituted the only truly American music from a nationalistic perspective. It's worth speculating a bit about how well this viewpoint dovetailed into Dvořák's own personal experience. Although he never discussed the issue at length as an ideological proposition, it's probably fair to say that he was a great patriot (that is, he loved his country and his heritage) but he despised nationalism (the assertion of one group's inherent superiority over others), of which he had been a victim, and struggled against, all his life.

Taking the African American/Native American side (musically, Dvořák made no distinction between the two) would have been, for him, second nature, as would be attempting to capture the spirit of these "Negro melodies" in his new symphony—with the proviso that he was not actually copying them any more than he copied Czech folk tunes. Remember that the fake spiritual "Goin' Home" came from the symphony, not the other way around, and that the main theme of the scherzo, supposedly inspired (like the slow movement) by a scene from Longfellow's *The Song of Hiawatha*, sounds suspiciously like the Slavonic Dance No. 7. On the other hand, having turned his back on Brahmsian orthodoxy in the Eighth Symphony, it perhaps suited Dvořák's purposes as a symphonist to allow listeners to think that his use of this specially constituted melodic material justifies the treatment that it receives here. In other words, the content to some extent explains the form.

Throughout his career, Dvořák had experimented with various kinds of cyclical construction (that is, shared themes between movements) as well as variation techniques to unify his symphonic structures. His first chamber works, as well as the very First Symphony, share themes and mottos between movements. The Second and Fourth Symphonies have first-movement introductions that appear, varied, at the beginning of each work's respective scherzo. The Fifth Symphony employs cyclical thematic recall in its outer movements and links the two inner ones through shared variations, while the Eighth is entirely based on the variation idea. So the cyclical procedures in the Ninth Symphony are not new, save for the degree to which Dvořák uses them.

The first movement's exposition contributes the principal motto themes. There are either one or two, depending on how you count them. After the introduction, the horns present the first subject, a question-and-answer tune beginning with a rising and falling arpeggio. After a full counterstatement, the second subject begins with a mirror theme (going up, then down) on the woodwinds, leading directly to a closing melody on solo flute (often assumed to have been inspired by the spiritual "Swing Low, Sweet Chariot"). More than its purported inspiration, this famous tune happens to be an inversion (that is, the upside-down form) of the horn phrase from the first subject. Both themes appear in all three remaining movements, so the symphony has either one musical motto or, if you consider this closing melody separately, two.

Dvořák also directs that the exposition be repeated, a practice he had given up in the previous two symphonies (three if you count his decision in connection with the Sixth). As in the scherzo of that same Sixth Symphony, he makes a special point here of framing the unusual melodic content within a severely traditional— even by this point somewhat old-fashioned—formal structure, driving home forcibly his point that this material, however unusual, has as much right to be used as part of a large classical design as any theme by Beethoven. For this reason, the exposition repeat should always be observed, particularly as it's also a relatively short and compact movement to begin with.

The famous largo, with its gorgeous brass chorale opening and rapt principal theme, the most famous solo ever written for English horn, should be left to speak for itself. Attempting to describe it is like trying to analyze the taste of a ripe peach. It exists in some sort of primal realm of musical being and is best enjoyed accordingly, in all of its pristine simplicity of utterance. The hardly less well-known scherzo, which adds a touch of brilliance in the form of a festive and difficult part for the triangle, may begin like a Slavonic Dance, but the central trio section has a tune that sounds mightily like "Over the River and Through the Woods, to Grandmother's House We Go." Although Dvořák seems to be heading in the direction of the first motto theme on the horns at the movement's end, the climax that arrives actually cuts to the second subject's closing melody— a particularly effective touch.

The finale opens with a march that turns into one of Dvořák's most graphic train tunes (the huffing and puffing continuation in triplets on the strings and horns). It skids to a halt with a particularly ear-catching impression of musically applying the brakes. It's worth mentioning in this connection that conductors particularly sensitive to Dvořák's late style will always have the single *mezzo forte* cymbal stroke played with a soft stick on a suspended cymbal. Not only is this one of his most characteristic percussion sonorities, it quite aptly sounds like a hiss of escaping steam. After a soulful secondary melody on the clarinets, the development reviews all the principal tunes from the previous three movements. These continue to pop up amid the formal recapitulation, which ultimately reaches a tremendous climax, consisting of the second movement's brass chorale accompanied by pounding timpani.

The mournful prelude to the coda and the ensuing grinding dissonances in the brass, produced by the collision of the main theme of the finale with the first movement's motto, offer the greatest surprise of all: this is actually a tragic finale, like the Seventh's. Even that very American-sounding boogie-woogie bass line and last-minute turn to the major key can't efface the sadness that lingers as the final chord fades slowly and gently to triple *piano*. Here is yet another case, as with so many works of Mozart, in which the music's sheer beauty and lovability makes it easy to forget just how emotionally expressive it really is. Dvořák wrote no symphonies after 1893, and it's difficult not to hear in this ending a nostalgic farewell to a genre that had served him honorably and to which he contributed so much.

The Concertos

Piano Concerto (1876)
Violin Concerto (1880)
Cello Concerto (1895)

Virtually every concerto composed during the romantic period was written either for the composer/performer's own private use or on commission by a specific virtuoso. None of Dvořák's was. This accounts for the fact that he only wrote three, each for a different solo instrument. It also explains their different approaches to form, their highly varied content, and their checkered performance history. He was under no constraints other than those he imposed on himself. I am not suggesting that Dvořák simply decided that God wanted him to write concertos and proceeded accordingly. He knew as well as anyone that if famous virtuosos played his pieces and added their illustrious names to his, it could only be a useful career move. It didn't exactly turn out that way, but in the long run it also didn't really matter, and music lovers can only be delighted that Dvořák decided to hedge his bets at least three times.

In the nineteenth century, there were basically two different kinds of concertos, distinguished by the structure of their opening movements and the way they handle the introduction of the solo voice into the musical discourse. The differences between these two types have been the subject of endless scholarly discussion; there's no need to do more than briefly summarize them here.

The first type, perhaps best known as the *classical concerto*, begins (sometimes after an opening gesture by the solo) with a long orchestral introduction that sets out the thematic exposition, but unlike in a purely orchestral work such as a symphony, there is no firm movement away from the home key for the second subject group. In fact, the second subject group isn't defined at all until the exposition gets repeated with the addition of the solo, which may add its own themes and finally does change key, thus establishing the terms of the ongoing dialogue with the orchestra. The effect of this on the first movement is to create the subtle impression of a musical discussion among equals, with both the orchestra and the soloist contributing necessary elements to their evolving discourse. This form was invented by Mozart and carried on by Beethoven, Brahms, and a few others.

Romantic concerto form, typified in most textbooks by the Mendelssohn Violin Concerto, usually begins straight away with the soloist. The orchestra has a more obviously accompanimental role, but it also provides important episodes of contrast in terms of color and dynamics. Because of the way that the composer introduces his soloist, the overall impression in these works is often one in which the solo seldom yields the spotlight. The need to balance the demands of virtuoso performers with the formal requirements of large-scale composition created a huge number of these concertos during the romantic period, mostly for piano and violin. It also led to a great deal of hybridization of first-movement forms, some imaginative and many simply inept.

Dvořák is virtually unique in the romantic period in that he was one of the very few great composers who was not a primarily a pianist. He also wrote successful concertos according to both the classical and romantic formal models, but there is a sense in which they all, irrespective of their first-movement forms, belong in the classical camp. Like Haydn before him and Sibelius after him, Dvořák's "instrument" was the orchestra as a whole. He was not by nature or temperament a virtuoso, and so his concertos, despite many flashy and exciting passages, tend to treat the orchestra and the soloist as equal participants in a joint endeavor.

Piano Concerto

Many hostile things have been said about this concerto. Among them: Dvořák, not being a virtuoso pianist himself (although he was a very good one), had no clue how to write for the instrument. The piece is formally dysfunctional. The relationship between the solo and orchestra is unsatisfactory, with the piano part too thin to hold its own against the heavy orchestration. Only Czech pianists play it, out of patriotic duty, and then only in an edition with a completely rewritten and more idiomatic solo part. Imagine, then, how surprising it is to discover in the work's original version a shapely, attractive, lyrical piece with no dead spots whatsoever, in which the interaction between the piano and orchestra has much of the typical give-and-take of the great classical concertos.

If Brahms recast the virtuoso romantic piano concerto in terms of classical forms, then it's fair to say that Dvořák did exactly the opposite: he offers a classical piano concerto presented in romantic style. There is no other work quite like it in the entire nineteenth-century repertoire for the instrument, and this alone explains why it has been so widely disparaged and misunderstood. Dvořák frankly admitted that he had no intention of writing a typical virtuoso work, and despite his willingness to revise when necessary, he did not touch a note once he heard it in performance. He knew he had done well, and beyond that, the piece was by no means a failure in his own lifetime, achieving success on several occasions both at home and abroad. So rather than complain about what the music is not, it pays to consider what in fact it is.

The first point to note is that although the piano is by far the most powerful solo instrument of the three that Dvořák wrote for, the orchestra he uses here is the smallest required by any of his concertos. In fact, the forces listed match those of Beethoven's and Mozart's concertos that include trumpets and timpani, and so explain why the piano has no problems making itself heard, despite the lack of padding and ornamental figuration in the part. But the resemblance goes deeper than the orchestration. Dvořák's concerto is a romantic homage to his beloved classical masters, a fascinating and witty mixture of forms and styles.

The opening theme is a soulful Slavic strain that rapidly builds to a passionate climax. The orchestra begins as if intent on playing an orthodox classical exposition. What happens next, though, sounds like a colorful journey backwards through concerto history. The orchestra doesn't get much farther before a dramatic, very Beethovenian crescendo leads to an abortive climax, and the piano interrupts with an entrance similar to that in the German composer's Fourth Piano Concerto. So there's no second subject at all until the orchestra and piano present it jointly, and it comes as an even bigger surprise because it's pure Mozart. Specifically, it sounds like a slightly distorted recollection of the second subject of *Eine Kleine Nachtmusik*'s first movement. In this context, its presence has both nostalgic charm and more than a dollop of Mozartian humor.

At about eighteen minutes, the movement isn't at all long for the first part of a concerto: substantially shorter than that of

Brahms's First Concerto, for example, and even a bit less lengthy than that of Beethoven's "Emperor" Concerto. So Dvořák has not overworked his ideas past their natural limits. The entire movement is drawn to scale, and the recapitulation presents the first and second subjects in their proper sequence as coherently as in any classical exemplar you might care to name. This is also the only Dvořák concerto to offer the soloist a genuine cadenza: a passage in improvisatory style for the piano alone based on the themes heard thus far. Here it has exactly the same function as in any classical concerto: to balance the purely orchestral opening. It's a short cadenza, appropriately, and fully written out (like the one in Beethoven's "Emperor" Concerto) rather than left to the pianist to improvise, and it sets the seal on the work's characterful homage to tradition.

The slow movement is breathtakingly beautiful, simple, and eloquent. It's a song in dialogue between piano and orchestra, and it has something of the dreamy atmosphere of Mozart's famous Piano Concerto No. 21 ("Elvira Madigan"). Mozartian too is the music's intimacy and the feeling of chamber music writ large. The tunes, though, are vintage Dvořák, and he does find room for one romantic outburst in the middle. But like all such moments in this concerto, the storm blows over quickly. In keeping with classical practice, the trumpets and drums remain silent throughout, but the writing for woodwinds is particularly captivating.

Dvořák loved to write themes with repeated notes. He opens the finale with a typical example of this habit, offering the opportunity for a little pianistic counterpoint while also contributing a three-note motive that quickly detaches itself as a sort of orchestral refrain between sections. A dancelike episode leads to the second subject: an exotic strain in Dvořák's best "Stranger in Paradise" mode, the rich harmony well suited to the parade of keys through which it passes. Formally, the movement is a

VC

combination of sonata and *rondo* (that is, ABACA, etc.) such as Mozart would have recognized.

Dvořák's Piano Concerto has been making a comeback both in concert and on recordings, particularly among specialists in the presentation of classical concertos and partisans of period-performance practice. This isn't at all surprising given its frame of reference. Nor has it been neglected by some of the more prominent members of the virtuoso school. It was a particular favorite of the late Sviatoslav Richter. If it will never be as popular as the more famous works of its era, this doesn't mean that the music is a failure. Its eclectic mixture of stylistic elements marks it out as one of Dvořák's most intellectually self-aware pieces: exactly what his music is not supposed to be. However, the fact that the Piano Concerto may not fit commonly held stereotypes about the composer need not prevent sympathetic listeners from enjoying its manifold charms.

Violin Concerto

Like the Piano Concerto, the Violin Concerto has had its share of detractors on formal grounds, but it has been enjoying a resurgence in popularity that is most welcome, as it happens to be one of the great works in the genre. Because Dvořák was himself a string player, it has never had to suffer the indignity of having its solo part rewritten by someone else, although its gestation was in fact quite complicated. He wrote the original version in around 1880, hoping that it would please the famous composer/virtuoso Joseph Joachim, for whom Brahms had written his own Violin Concerto. Joachim was, if anything, even stricter a classicist than was Brahms, as his own works in the form clearly show (Joachim's attractive "Hungarian" Concerto still hovers on the fringes of the repertoire).

Always ready to oblige an artist whom he respected, Dvořák rewrote the work completely after receiving Joachim's comments and then undertook a further thorough revision of the violin part of this second version. However, when it was suggested that he make a third major structural revision, Dvořák dug in his heels. Joachim in fact never played the work, and this tacit snub has haunted it ever since. The principal bone of contention concerns, as should come as no surprise, the form of the first movement. It begins like a virtuoso concerto of the Mendelssohn school, with the soloist taking center stage right from the beginning. Dvořák then adds an additional complication in that the movement isn't complete in and of itself. After a recapitulation of the first subject, it segues smoothly into the slow movement without pause. He was particularly satisfied with this decision, which achieves two desirable goals.

First, he keeps the concerto to a very modest length while enhancing its movement-to-movement continuity. At a touch over thirty minutes in most performances, the entire work lasts only a bit longer than the first movement alone of the Brahms Concerto or Joachim's own "Hungarian" Concerto (which ironically is almost never played without substantial cuts in its purely orchestral passages). Dvořák refused to heed the suggestion that he should go back and "complete" the first movement. In a letter to his publisher, he pointed out that this would increase the length of the movement by about a third, and that he felt comfortable with the shape of the work as it stood, save for a few small adjustments to the finale.

Second, Dvořák's first-movement gambit makes the delicious and energetic finale the focal point of the entire work, which is only fair, as it's probably one of the most successful and memorable finales in any violin concerto. The result is a perfectly balanced composition having three movements of virtually identical length, none of which outstays its welcome.

VC

It also saves the best for last, which is more than you can say for many of its romantic brethren. Unlike the Piano Concerto, the work contains a large share of virtuoso fireworks (although it contains no cadenza for the soloist in any movement), but this stems from the fact that a solo violin always needs to sound much busier than a piano if it is to stand out effectively against the full orchestra—in this case, one larger by two horns than its predecessor.

A work this well crafted and polished needs little in the way of verbal description. All of its principal themes come from Dvořák's top drawer, including the soulful principal tune of the first movement. The beginning of that infamous non-recapitulation is particularly excitingly managed, and the transition to the adagio is exquisite. Timpani are silent in the central slow movement, but the trumpets make a single dramatic and devastatingly effective appearance at its center. Dvořák's scoring, particularly for the wind section, sensitively frames the ornately lyrical solo writing. Indeed, the entire work really is a marvel of euphony throughout. The finale is full of rhythmic games for both solo and orchestra, with the violinist given a chance to dance with each section of the orchestra in turn, even including at one point a marvelous duet with solo timpani. Note the brilliant presentation of the opening theme, featuring the soloist framed by a magical musical halo from the full violin section softly playing the same melody.

With a rush to the finish guaranteed to bring a concert audience to its feet, this concerto has always been a favorite of the world's great violinists. Most of them—including such illustrious names as Milstein, Stern, Perlman, and Oistrakh—have recorded it. The work understandably enjoys the special advocacy of the composer's own great-grandson, the celebrated Czech violinist Joseph Suk, and so maintains a secure niche in the repertoire.

Cello Concerto

Few works dominate their genre the way Dvořák's Cello Concerto does. No other concerto for the instrument even comes close in size, expressive depth, melodic richness, and formal perfection. For most cellists it represents Mecca, the Wailing Wall, and the Vatican all rolled into one. Taken along with the Bach Cello Suites, it defines the career of the modern virtuoso. Indeed, it can be said to have played a large role in actually giving legitimacy to the very idea of a solo cellist as a modern virtuoso with a repertoire all his or her own. It spawned countless later works in the same genre, from Elgar to Shostakovich and beyond. This was the piece that caused Brahms to gasp with admiration and lament the fact that he had not written it himself, thus tabling once and for all any question of formal inadequacy, despite the work's being every bit as unorthodox as Dvořák's other two concertos.

The Cello Concerto also has two other big things going for it. It triumphantly concludes the glorious series of works that constitute Dvořák's "American" period (1893–95), when he occupied the position of Director of the National Conservatory in New York. It shares with its companion pieces—including the "New World" Symphony, the "American" Quartet, the String Quintet Op. 97, and the Humoresques, for piano—a melodic inspiration clearly drawn from Negro spirituals and American popular song, while at the same time always sounding inimitably Slavic and totally like Dvořák. It also (and this is really important) has genuine autobiographical significance, giving commentators something to write about, besides tonal relationships and formal strategies, that is endearing, true, and indicative of what the music "means" in a wider sense.

Specifically, when working on the slow movement, Dvořák learned that his sister-in-law Josefina was gravely ill. She had been his first love back in the 1860s, and he composed a song cycle called *Cypresses* expressing his feelings for her. These pieces have an interesting history, later being arranged for string quartet and revised as the Love Songs, Op. 83. At the same time as Dvořák was arranging their German edition, he asked his translator for some texts in that language, and she produced what became the Four Songs, Op. 82, the first of which, "Leave Me Alone," was a favorite of Josefina's. Dvořák incorporated it into the slow movement of this concerto. Josefina died shortly thereafter, at which time Dvořák further revised the finale, creating a sweetly nostalgic, wistful coda recalling both the main theme of the first movement and another bit of the song. The revision, however personal in meaning, fulfills a purely musical function as well. Even in his grief, Dvořák was too smart a composer to ignore that aspect.

Knowledge of these extramusical facts is not a prerequisite for fully enjoying this great work. But we do know them, and it's undeniable that they have helped add to the music's mystique over time. It may surprise you to learn that this work is actually Dvořák's second in the genre. There's an early Cello Concerto in A Major from the mid-1860s that exists complete in draft form, arranged for cello and piano. It was orchestrated in the early decades of the twentieth century and is virtually unknown (although it has been recorded and really isn't at all bad). Still, no one would mistake that early work for this one when referring to *the* Dvořák Cello Concerto. I mention it here to avoid confusion if you happen to see this one referred to by some smart-alec as "No. 2," which happens from time to time.

The most remarkable thing about this piece, aside from the fact that it positively overflows with beautiful melody, is its orchestration. Dvořák writes for an ensemble larger than that of any of his other concertos. For example, I have already pointed out how in the Piano and Violin Concertos, the slow movements left out timpani and minimized or eliminated the trumpets as well. Here they appear in all three movements, and this is the only concerto of the three to include trombones, tuba, piccolo, and triangle, all used with singular aptness and gusto. Miraculously, there's absolutely no feeling of inhibition, that the presence of the comparatively reticent solo instrument has put a damper on the power of the full orchestra—quite the opposite, in fact.

Nevertheless, despite these large forces and Dvořák's delight in turning them loose, you won't find a hint of bombast anywhere. Note, for example, the presence of three horns instead of the usual four. Dvořák treats them as a genuine trio at the opening of the finale and most magically at the return of the principal theme of the slow movement after the tempestuous middle section. The second subject of the first movement has also become famous all by itself as one of the most gorgeous passages ever written for solo horn. The tone of the cello, often dark and lacking in penetration, has inspired Dvořák to devise the most colorful and varied accompaniments imaginable so as to spotlight the soloist in the most effective way possible.

Listen to the beginning of the slow movement, in which the cello communes first with high woodwinds (flutes and oboes primarily), then with clarinets and trombones. Pages of score go by without the participation of the violins at all. The most poetic single moment occurs in the finale's revised epilogue, Dvořák's memorial to Josefina, with its muted trumpets and horns. It powerfully reveals one of his greatest gifts: the ability to write music of exceptional sweetness without ever sounding excessively sentimental or saccharine. For a composer of the romantic period, where heart-on-sleeve emotionalism often risks self-parody, there really is nothing more important, expressively speaking.

In the Cello Concerto, Dvořák's orchestral wizardry operates hand in hand with his formal ingenuity, most famously when he omits the opening theme from the first-movement recapitulation entirely (saving it for the coda), proceeding instead to a triumphant statement of the second subject in the home key (that lovely horn solo, now in the full orchestra). A step universally lauded as an original stroke of genius, many commentators fail to realize that Dvořák exploits exactly the same effect in the first movements of his First and Third Symphonies. This concerto also provides further evidence of Dvořák's resistance to suggestions that he felt violated his artistic intentions. The cellist for whom he wrote it suggested a virtuoso cadenza at the end of the finale, which annoyed Dvořák so much that he was not disappointed to conduct the London premiere with another player entirely.

The manifold excellence of the Cello Concerto, its originality and perfection of form and content, has cast a long shadow over Dvořák's other two concertos. This isn't entirely fair. The opportunity to write a work of such originality, one that effectively defines a new medium, only occurs to most artists rarely, if at all, over the course of a lifetime. While music lovers are certainly justified in celebrating Dvořák's perspicacity in seizing the opportunity that this work presented him, there is no rational reason why anyone needs to neglect the Piano Concerto or the Violin Concerto simply because they aren't as obviously special. Each constitutes a distinguished contribution to its respective repertoire, a fact that, fortunately, is increasingly acknowledged as time passes.

Operas

Alfred (1870)
The King and the Charcoal Burner (1871, rev. 1874, 1887)
The Stubborn Lovers (1874)
Vanda (1875)
The Cunning Peasant (or *Šelma Sedlák*) (1877)
Dimitrij (1882, rev. 1895)
The Jacobin (or *Jakobin*) (1888, rev. 1897)
The Devil and Kate (1899)
Rusalka (1900)
Armida (1903)

This chapter attempts to answer the musical question: How can anyone not love a series of operas, one of which stars a chubby, unattractive, loud-mouthed spinster (*The Devil and Kate*) and another of which features a crooked villain named Adolf (*The Jacobin*)?

Dvořák has always had a bum rap as an opera composer, even in his own lifetime. There are many reasons for this, and I will consider in some detail the most important of them, because an understanding of popular misconceptions about his operatic output is critical to any appreciation of what he actually achieved. However, the whole subject boils down to a single basic problem already quite evident in Dvořák's day: an unwillingness to accept the possibility that any composer after Mozart could be equally adept at both theatrical and absolute music, at both opera and symphony. This wholly artificial and musically irrelevant line of demarcation arose from the late-nineteenth-century conflict between the Brahms and Wagner camps, a real musical war that produced feelings on both sides of exceptional intolerance and viciousness. Beyond that, there's the historical tendency of most composers to concentrate in one field or the other.

The persistence of this perspective has exercised a baleful influence on critical reaction to the work of numerous composers besides Dvořák, the most obvious being Tchaikovsky. But whereas in Tchaikovsky's case, the general acceptance of some of his operas and ballets leads to an undervaluation of his symphonies, the situation with Dvořák is reversed: admiration of the symphonies leads to neglect of the operas, a more easily maintained state of affairs, thanks to issues of language as well as the huge cost and logistical barriers opposing the entry of neglected works into the international repertoire. It has to be said in this connection that not all eleven of Dvořák's efforts are equally good. Indeed, I can't really say anything about the very first, *Alfred*, because it's never been published or recorded. The original overture (known as the *Dramatic Overture* or *Tragic Overture*), however, exists as an independent orchestral piece, and I discuss it accordingly in chapter 6.

The only way to really judge an opera's viability is to listen to the whole thing and, even better, to see it sympathetically staged. Absent that, no firm assessment is possible. Instead, commentators too frequently offer cheap, facile pot shots that replace the experience of seeing an actual performance with generic criticism of the libretto—almost invariably according to inapplicable literary standards that they are even less qualified to discuss authoritatively than they are the music itself. In reality, even operatic "specialist" composers typically write many more works than routinely get performed. Wagner's early operas are almost totally ignored, and if it weren't for complete *Ring* cycles, we'd hardly ever hear *Siegfried*. Mozart wrote approximately a dozen major operas that no one especially cares about today. The neglected output of famous names such as Rossini, Donizetti, Massenet, Rimsky-Korsakov, Tchaikovsky, Richard Strauss, and Verdi is far larger than the number of popular works. We even relegate to the fringes of the repertoire almost half the output of so popular a composer as Puccini, and there's a large group who fall into the category of "one shot wonders," led off by Mascagni and Leoncavallo and including Saint-Säens, Gounod, Weber, and most famously, Bizet.

Fair or not, this situation reflects the brutal reality of the operatic world, the embodiment of artistic Darwinism at its most elemental. It's a messy business, in which the sheer length and practical complexity of the medium often collide with the warring whims of impresarios, singers, stage directors, and conductors. Whole swaths of the repertoire can get sidelined for decades due to a dearth of vocalists able to take the lead roles, returning just as suddenly if conditions become favorable. There is no such thing as a perfect operatic masterpiece, if this means (as with so much purely instrumental music) an inviolable text in which every note is sacrosanct. Even were it not for the misunderstandings, the issues of language, and the editorial problems produced by Dvořák's multiple revisions of certain works, the genre itself is inherently heterogeneous, resisting easy categorization.

Despite this daunting reality, one of Dvořák's operas, *Rusalka*, has recently made it to the international stage, where it has been strikingly successful. It beggars belief that the composer of this masterpiece only had a single great work in him, and now that almost all of them have been recorded, it's at least possible for you to hear them at home and draw your own conclusions. More importantly, if you enjoy Dvořák generally—his style and sound—then you will certainly delight in getting to know these operas, because whatever the ultimate judgment of history may be regarding their stageworthiness, they are all full of characteristic music and gratifyingly personal in style. Most people familiar with them at least agree on this last point.

Like Mozart, Dvořák was a human sponge, soaking up inspiration wherever he found it and melding it into his own idiom. Paradoxically, this adaptability seldom manifests itself in blatant imitation, because he wielded it within the context of an artistic personality so strong and so gifted in its store of melodic ideas that he almost never felt the need to copy anyone directly. In those instances where he does borrow some obvious stylistic or technical device, he makes absolutely no effort to disguise the fact—imitation being, for him, not just the sincerest form of flattery but also a way of demonstrating his awareness of the larger world and asserting his (and by association, Czech music's) right of equal participation.

This may sound fine in theory, but to put matters on a firmer footing, I offer from the accompanying CDs (disc 1, tracks 5 and 6) an extract from act 2 of *The Devil and Kate*, a true gem of a comic opera. The action takes place in hell (that's right: hell), to whence the rather coarse and irritating heroine has been transported by the bumbling devil of the title. The prelude (track 5) begins and ends with a comic send-up of the subterranean Nibelheim music from Wagner's *Das Rheingold* (which Wagner himself possibly got from the scherzo of Schubert's *Death and the Maiden* string quartet, but that's another story). The lovely middle section is pure Dvořák, the theme representing the shepherd Jirka who has agreed to rescue Kate. The act then begins (track 6) with a lively chorus of card-playing devils that strikingly evokes in spirit and mood, if not in actual melody, the similar opening, also in hell (the Greek one this time) to the fourth tableau of Offenbach's *Orpheus in the Underworld*.

Wagner and Offenbach: an unlikely mixture and one that would surely have horrified both, even as it baffles most commentators, although Dvořák knew them equally and intimately well. On closer examination, however, it becomes clear that this is only the beginning of a particularly rich and flavorsome musical recipe. The one ingredient that everyone acknowledges is Wagner, whose influence on Dvořák (both early and late) is real, if often overstated. From the biographical point of view, it stems, as already mentioned in the discussion of the symphonies, from that single Prague concert in the early 1860s that Wagner conducted and in which Dvořák played. And yet, he also participated in quite literally hundreds upon hundreds of opera performances as part of his regular job at the Provisional Theater, with hardly a word ever mentioned about the possible influence of that music on Dvořák's own works in the genre. This situation is ridiculous, particularly as there's no great mystery as to what he actually heard and performed.

On the following page, I offer a table listing the top ten works and composers in the repertoire of the Provisional Theater starting in 1862, when it was founded and Dvořák joined the orchestra. Not a single work by Wagner was played there, incidentally, although Dvořák certainly knew Wagner's early operas (see "Dvořák Timeline" for the dates of their Prague premieres), and he had the opportunity of both playing in them and seeing them at the competing German-language company just a few blocks away. He particularly loved the *Tannhäuser* overture, as the Third and Fourth Symphonies, along with the *Dramatic Overture* (to *Alfred*) demonstrate. The point that needs stressing, though, is that in order to evaluate honestly and fairly the sources of Dvořák's operatic style, it's necessary to know what he knew and hear what he heard.

As the table clearly shows, what he heard was overwhelmingly Italian and French. Much of the purported influence attributed to Wagner can actually be traced back to Parisian grand opera, Meyerbeer in particular, since he served as a principal source of inspiration for the German composer as well. Indeed, the

Prague Provisional Theater Opera Repertoire: 1862–1883

	Ten Most Popular Works*				Ten Most Popular Composers		
Rank	Composer	Work	No. Times Performed	Year of First Performance	Composer	No. Works Performed	Total Performances
1	Gounod	Faust	121	1867	Offenbach	19	405
2	Smetana	The Bartered Bride	116	1866	Smetana	8	265
3	Verdi	Il Trovatore	114	1863	Verdi	6	261
4	Meyerbeer	Les Huguenots	78	1864	Suppé	9	189
5	Offenbach	Les Brigands	77	1870	Lecoq	12	188
6	Auber	La Muette de Portici	76	1863	Meyerbeer	5	184
7	Offenbach	Orpheus in the Underworld	64	1863	Gounod	3	169
8	Rossini	The Barber of Seville	62	1863	Donizetti	10	160
9	Rossini	William Tell	58	1866	Auber	10	159
10	Meyerbeer	Robert le Diable	57	1864	Rossini	5	149

* works with first performances during Dvořák's tenure (1862–1871)

Source: Daily Repertoire of the Provisional Theatre Opera in Prague, by Jan Smaczny. *Miscellanea musicologica*, vol. XXXIV, Prague 1994.

descending brass proclamations in the prelude to Meyerbeer's *Robert le diable* reveal a possible kinship to the similar writing in Dvořák's act 2 prelude to *The Devil and Kate*. The Meyerbeer opera, composed and premiered in 1831 yet all but unknown today, chalked up approximately 600 performances in Paris alone between its opening and 1868. It reached the stage of the Provisional Theater in 1864 and enjoyed fifty-seven repetitions over the next two decades, half of them during Dvořák's tenure there. The delicious blasphemy of the famous "Cloister" scene in act 3 in which Bertram (a.k.a. Satan) resurrects a batch of dead nuns to seduce Robert—accompanied by the descending brass gestures of the prelude—exercised a fascination on more than a few composers of the age.

The other Meyerbeer opera of singular relevance to both Dvořák and Smetana is *Dinorah*, a hugely popular piece in its day. Sometimes mockingly referred to as "a dead opera about a live goat," the story is silly and contrived beyond imagining, and there's probably no way it could be successfully revived. The act 2 "Shadow Song," however, remains a sometime recital item among coloratura sopranos. Much of the music is very good, and like all Meyerbeer, it is superbly crafted and theatrically effective. More to the point, the work is not a grand opera at all but a pastoral comedy. Its cast of superstitious but jolly villagers, bagpipers, shepherds, and other rustic characters validated at a stroke the basic dramaturgy of the Czech "village opera." *Dinorah* reached the Prague Provisional Theater in 1863 and was performed more than a dozen times during Dvořák's tenure. Smetana's *The Bartered Bride* had its premiere three years later, and the rest, as they say, is history.

Another missing link worth mentioning is Berlioz, a composer whom everyone tends to ignore because his originality is supposed to be so unique that it couldn't possibly have rubbed off on anyone else. Nevertheless, his music took Prague by storm on his visit there in 1846, and his impact on the imaginations of European composers (especially in Germany and Austria) in the decades before the rise of Wagner was considerable. As I noted in connection with the Second Symphony, Smetana conducted Berlioz's *Roméo et Juliette* in Prague in 1864, and there's certainly something of the French composer's general orchestral and rhythmic brilliance in Dvořák's output.

Wherever one chooses to draw the line on the "influence" question, it is abundantly clear that Dvořák knew, intimately and well, vastly more operatic repertoire than virtually anyone who studies or writes about him. Just how experienced was he? Altogether the Provisional Theater during the twenty-one years of its existence featured approximately 210 operas by seventy-two composers of Italian, French, German, Czech/Slavic, and Russian extraction (not including those by Dvořák himself). Its work load was staggering. The company offered twelve to fifteen shows per month on average, all year round. That equates to something on the order of 1,296 to 1,620 performances in which Dvořák could have participated during his nine years in the orchestra pit, excluding the freelance jobs that he took at the same time.

Obviously, Dvořák didn't play in every performance of every work. Nor, in considering the question of influence and inspiration, do we know what he thought of them all. There must have been plenty that he liked and just as many that he loathed (especially as a violist). But when all is said and done—taking into consideration the music he actually performed, the productions he could have seen both in Czech at the Provisional Theater and elsewhere in German (which he spoke), and also his personal encounters with other composers and opportunities for private study—there's no question that Dvořák had about as useful, practical, and culturally diverse an experience of opera as any composer in history who has ever written one.

Alfred

The King and the Charcoal Burner

Dvořák's first opera, an epic story of conflict between Britain and Denmark based on a German libretto, reveals the extent of his ambition to achieve notoriety beyond the borders of his homeland. This, however, is about all that can be said about it, because it's never been recorded or published. Professor Jan Smaczny—the acknowledged authority on Dvořák's operas and holder of the Hamilton Harty Chair of Music at Queen's University, Belfast—has expressed the view both in print and to this author that the influence of Wagner on this work has been somewhat exaggerated, and given all the foregoing, I'm not a bit surprised.

On the other hand, Dvořák himself admitted with typical honesty that the first version of *The King and the Charcoal Burner* had availed itself of some Wagnerian characteristics, but then he scrapped the entire work and reset the libretto to new music, substantially revising the opera once again in the late 1880s. So there are in fact two Dvořák operas with the same name, the same story, and completely different music, and for this reason it's said that he wrote eleven operas, even though there are only ten titles. Once again, until critical editions of the scores and, more importantly, complete recordings become available, there's no way to discuss the opera meaningfully. Based on the recorded extracts that are available, which sound just like the Dvořák we know and love, the definitive version likely contains plenty of fine music. The overture, as might be expected, is delightful. Whether an opera with such an unresonant title, on the other hand, stands a ghost of chance on the international stage is another matter.

The Stubborn Lovers

You may encounter the name of this work in its antediluvian form: *The Pig-Headed Peasants*. It's hard not to forgive anyone under those circumstances for avoiding it like the plague. This absolutely wonderful, bright and breezy one-acter was not a success in Dvořák's lifetime, a fact sometimes used to explain why it should be ignored now. Of course, people also ignore *The Cunning Peasant*, which was tremendously successful in Dvořák's lifetime, so contemporary popularity does not and should not count for much in evaluating these works today.

Lasting all of about seventy-five minutes (including a ten-minute overture eminently worthy of independent performance), *The Stubborn Lovers* has the distinction of being the first Czech comic opera set to continuous music (Smetana's first examples had dialogue, later converted to recitative). Dvořák's symphonic credentials are very much in evidence in the way the brief arias and ensembles are embedded in the ongoing musical flow, but beyond that, it's difficult not to hear the composer's huge experience with operetta, Offenbach especially, in the music's lightness and effervescence. Everything is drawn to scale, there's no overreaching, heaviness, or excess. As a one-act attraction, this would make a fine double bill with another single-act comedy, such as Puccini's *Gianni Schicchi* or perhaps Ravel's equally rarely heard *L'heure espagnole*.

The story is simplicity itself: two meddlesome single parents, a widow and a widower, want their children to get married. The kids are indeed fond of each other, but they hate the thought of being pushed around by their elders. Meanwhile the godfather of both, understanding the situation and unwilling to let the two parents mess things up, decides to get the youngsters together by making them jealous. So he starts a rumor that that each of them is actually the object of affection of the other's parent. This naturally makes them furious and causes a fine ruckus among the villagers, and so the two lovers are eventually forced to admit their feelings, and the situation sorts itself out in the end. It's a slender story, granted, but only if drawn out of proportion, and it's a tribute to Dvořák's much-maligned dramatic instincts that his setting matches its subject perfectly.

On CD 1, track 7, you can hear the young girl Lenka's aria, which translates more or less as "What's the matter with me?" In it she describes her confusion on realizing that she has feelings for young Toník only because she believes that he's wanted by someone else. In a bit more than three minutes, Dvořák captures the freshness of young love, with its sudden mood swings, frustrations, and hopes for future happiness. The music exudes a spontaneous warmth of feeling. If you want to dip your toes gingerly into the world of Dvořák's operas without investing too much time and money up front, *The Stubborn Lovers* offers an excellent place to start.

Vanda

Vanda is a big, juicy grand opera that I have no doubt could create a sensation in live performance. It has a bit of everything: conflicts between love and duty, Germans and Poles (nothing new there), heathens and Christians, nobility and commoners. There's a royal coronation, a solemn temple scene, a fateful oath to the pagan gods, two duels, a major battle, and an entire black-magic act, complete with a maniacal dancing sorceress and mystical incantations. The choruses (there are a lot of them) are particularly spectacular. It's really something of a miracle that Dvořák was able to cram all this into about two and three-quarter hours, and the charge of excessive length just won't fly here. The piece is simply exciting as hell, with virtually nonstop action spread over five jam-packed acts. The main roles in the love triangle forming the basis of the plot (Princess Vanda; her lover, the low-born Polish knight Slavoj; and the German Prince Roderick) are all effectively characterized, and their more lyrical scenes well placed in the overall scheme.

The story, in a nutshell, is that Vanda loves Slavoj even though he is not of noble birth. He is, however, the best knight in town, and when she becomes queen (despite her misgivings), he easily defeats all challengers, to the dismay of the stuffy high priest. The happiness of the two lovers is forestalled, permanently as it turns out, by the arrival of the German Prince Roderick, who demands Vanda's hand in marriage to cement an alliance between their peoples. She hesitates for the next two acts, searching for a way out of her dilemma (including the use of black magic), and in the process twice saves Roderick from defeat in single combat at the hands of Slavoj. The humiliated German accordingly sends his forces into battle against Vanda's smaller and weaker army. On the verge of a catastrophic loss, she appears in the temple— blood-soaked, sword in hand—and swears to the gods that if the Poles triumph, her life will be forfeit. The gods take her at her word: the Poles win (miraculously within seconds), and the next morning, Vanda and Slavoj bid each other a sad farewell, after which, to the sound of shimmering strings and rippling harp, she ecstatically throws herself into the river and drowns. The people lament.

Now what's not to like about that? The problem with *Vanda* lies not in the music, the story, or the libretto itself, but in the contemporary disdain for grand opera in general: its conventions; its love of spectacle for its own sake—being grandiose and splashy and merely entertaining and, in general, giving the audience maximum bang for its buck—even at the expense of theoretically higher cultural values. Indeed, the remarkable thing about *Vanda* is not its uncertainties or absurdities, which are in fact surprisingly few given its genre, but rather the sheer confidence and gusto of the music, obviously the result of Dvořák's experience in the opera house. Perhaps when the critical edition gets around to issuing the full score in the next few decades, this opera will have a chance to make its case before the public. As grand operas go, you could do much worse.

The Cunning Peasant

Your reaction to this opera will depend to a certain extent on how you feel about the word *peasant*. Operas of all periods are full of them, and music lovers tend to fall into two categories when confronted with their presence: those who enjoy cute, stylized representations of simple country folk and welcome a break from the intensity of the main story line, and those seriously annoyed at cute, stylized representations of simple country folk because they interrupt the action and water down the intensity of the main story line. The latter view probably predominates, particularly in today's fast-paced and impatient world.

It's worth remembering, then, that because Dvořák was proud of his own peasant roots, his view of this particular class was not condescending, and more to the point, his characterization of them is generally sympathetic and realistic. They are not usually foolish bumpkins running around in colorful native costumes looking ethnic and wasting valuable time best spent on plot development (as they largely are in Meyerbeer's *Dinorah*, for example). On the contrary: they are normal people who happen to live in small country towns and villages. In considering operas like this one, the comedy does not arise from poking fun at a particular social class but rather always from the dramatic situation. Of course, this may be silly all by itself, but that's another matter entirely.

Martin, a wealthy farmer, has a sexy daughter (let's call her Betty to avoid all those inconvenient Czech diacritical marks). Betty is in love with a poor nobody named Jeník, but Martin wants to marry her off to the doltish son of another rich farmer. Meanwhile, the Prince spots Betty and goes after her too (as does his wife's valet, Jean). With the connivance of the clever village headwoman Veruna (every village has one), Betty gets the Prince to promise Jeník a prime piece of land if she agrees to—well, you know. Meanwhile, Veruna gets the Princess and the Princess's chambermaid, Berta (who loves Jean), to dress up as Betty, making for three identical girls who, of course, confront their respective significant others. The abashed Prince ultimately gives Jeník the land anyway so that he and Betty can get married, and the couples pair off appropriately at the end.

Yes, it's dumb, but the test of all such stories is not the thrilling plot but rather the wealth of characterization and the quality of the musical setting. There are some really beautiful arias and ensembles (such as the Prince's act 1 aria and the same act's concluding quartet for the four women), and once again Dvořák has drawn the drama skillfully to scale. He refuses to lay on the local color too thickly, the adorable choruses of villagers do their bit and get out of the way with dispatch, and the opera's two acts last less than two hours—much less if one discounts the ten-minute-long overture (which became popular independently in Dvořák's lifetime and deserves to be so again). In short, the music has all of the composer's typical richness of invention and easy continuity.

So what's the problem? Simple. It's not Smetana's *The Bartered Bride*. In Dvořák's own lifetime, this wasn't an issue: more of the same was exactly what people wanted, at least in Central Europe. Today, though, there seems to be room for only one Czech "village opera" in the international repertoire, and the public has chosen well. Smetana's work, although not quite as compact or skillfully assembled, has a more interesting and less contrived plot, wittier situations, and greater depth of musical characterization—in short, it's a better opera altogether. This doesn't mean that *The Cunning Peasant* is bad. It's simply that in the world of opera, coming in a clear second to an internationally recognized masterpiece is almost a guaranteed ticket to oblivion. So this lovely, charming piece will most likely remain a guilty pleasure for hard-core Dvořák enthusiasts, and there's nothing at all wrong with that.

Dimitrij

Dimitrij is a masterpiece, a grand opera on Verdian lines. As the "Dvořák Timeline" shows, the Italian master's *Aida* appeared in Prague in 1875. There's little doubt that Dvořák was familiar with the work. The two composers have much in common, not least a basic honesty and directness of expression over and above any purely stylistic differences between them. In *Dimitrij*, Dvořák created a work that combines *Aida*'s orchestral finesse and four-act structure with *Don Carlo*'s depth of characterization and political dimension. Unfortunately, the textual situation more closely resembles the confused state of the latter than it does the former.

Dvořák knew he had done something special here, and he regarded *Dimitrij* as his best chance to score an international success—so much so that he was willing to do almost anything to achieve it. This meant a complete recomposition in the mid-1890s, but subsequent performances persuaded him that his first thoughts, by and large, remained the best. Just before his death, he authorized performances of the original combined with the revised third act. The only available recording returns to the first version of 1882–85, and it triumphantly vindicates Dvořák's initial conception, although to be fair, no one has heard or seen the later rewrite in over a hundred years. Practically speaking, the biggest issue facing any production of *Dimitrij* is finding a tenor who can sing the title role—murderously long and tiring both physically and emotionally, but also an extraordinary piece of musical characterization.

The plot may come as a surprise, as it follows directly the story told in Mussorgsky's *Boris Godunov*, which Dvořák evidently did not know at the time of composition. After the death of Czar Boris, the Polish armies of the pretender Dimitrij conquer Russia. He truly believes himself to be the long-lost son of Ivan the Terrible and Marfa, the Czarina. Only Dimitrij's Polish wife Marina knows the truth: that he is actually the child of a peasant, raised to realize Poland's dreams of conquest. In act 1, he presents himself to the Russian people and persuades Marfa to accept him as her legitimate child. The crowd, having acknowledged him as czar, turns on the surviving family of Boris and murders his wife and young son Fyodor, whose claim to the throne is upheld by the boyars, led by Prince Shuisky. Only Boris's daughter Xenia escapes the carnage, finding shelter with the prince.

The second act, the first half of which takes place during a grand ball at which Russians and Poles express their mutual loathing, reveals Marina as a scheming troublemaker who loves the throne more than she does her husband. In its second half, Xenia has been pursued to the catacombs by her family's murderers, only to be rescued by Dimitrij. They fall in love, although they are unaware of each other's identities. The act concludes as Dimitrij, hidden in the catacombs, overhears Shuisky's conspiracy to unseat him. He reveals himself to the conspirators, wins most of them over to his side, and condemns Shuisky to death. In act 3, the executions are about to go forward, but Xenia begs for mercy. Both Xenia and Dimitrij are shocked to realize with whom they were actually dealing down in the catacombs, but Dimitrij nevertheless pardons Shuisky. Marina, correctly perceiving the reason for this act of clemency, has a furious argument (in the form of a thrilling duet) with her husband and spits out the story of who he truly is. Although she regrets her words and claims to love him still, Dimitrij spurns her in horror, unsure whether or not to believe her.

In the last act, Dimitrij and Xenia declare their love, and Marina arranges to have her revenge: the girl is stabbed to death (a scene that Dvořák was asked to delete as a precondition to having the opera performed in Vienna). Shuisky, Dimitrij, and the people discover the crime and exclaim that the murderer must be apprehended. Marina is captured and confesses, at the same time revealing to the shocked populace Dimitrij's real identity. Marfa is asked this time to swear before God that Dimitrij truly is her son, but he stops her from committing blasphemy and so acknowledges the fraud. Shuisky shoots him dead on the spot, and the people lament the passing of a decent man who they now understand would have been a good czar because he truly cared for them.

Such a complex plot obviously requires time, a bit more than three hours (basically the same length as *Don Carlo*), but Dvořák sustains the drama extremely well. The opera is full of memorable scenes, not the least of which are Dimitrij's big duets with the three main female characters, each of whom is clearly delineated and fully developed musically. The role of Marina is particularly effective, combining the jealous pride of Verdi's Amneris (*Aida*), the vanity of Princess Eboli (*Don Carlo*), and perhaps also a touch of Lady Macbeth's scheming vindictiveness. The Czarina Marfa's two crucial appearances, at the beginning and end of the opera, effectively reveal her ongoing struggle between desire for vengeance on the murderers of her infant son and husband,

and her equally strong understanding of the need for a peaceful succession for the benefit of all. Hers is a truly noble portrait, and it fulfills an important structural function as well, framing the action of the drama.

Xenia's chief emotion, understandably, is fear, combined with the tormented knowledge that she loves the man indirectly responsible for her family's murder. Dvořák gives musical voice to these feelings with great sensitivity and lyrical beauty in her act 4 aria "I dreamed that death touched me with her right hand" (CD 1, track 8). The recurrent refrain of "Alas, alas" (in Czech, "*Běda, běda*") makes this aria a sort of Slavic equivalent to Leonora's "Pace, pace mio Dio" in Verdi's *La forza del destino*, similarly the expression of a tormented soul seeking peace. The aria's orchestral prelude may owe something in its nocturnal atmosphere to the opening of the "Nile" scene in *Aida*, but the harmony, rhythm, and orchestral coloration are all intensely Slav and vintage Dvořák.

Dimitrij himself must be counted one of the great tragic figures in nineteenth-century opera. Like many such characters in world literature, he is a good man trapped in a situation not of his own making, an unwitting tool of a plot that began when he was still an infant. In the last scene, when he finally comes to understand the truth, he accepts death rather than allowing further harm to come to the people he has sworn to protect. The opera's conclusion is not merely powerful and moving, it accomplishes exactly what all good grand operas should: the delivery of a larger political and moral message in the human terms of the principal character's personal tragedy. In sum, there is nothing in Dimitrij that falls below the highest musical and dramatic standards in a work of this type. Unlucky though it was, Dvořák was right to be proud of it, and I wouldn't be at all surprised if posterity ultimately confirms him in his view.

The Jacobin

The Jacobin is Dvořák's most Mozartian opera, in that it's a serious work in comic dress. Mozartian too is the subtlety of characterization, in which all the important roles are psychologically real, fully developed participants in a plausible drama. Yes, it takes place in a Czech village, but that's not really the point. The opera is not about "the village." The rustic setting and the usual subplot (about a rich old codger who wants to marry a young girl who already has a boyfriend her own age) take a back seat to a story of love in its wider manifestations: between father and son, husband and wife, and father and daughter. There's also love of art, of music in particular, and of one's own country, a political dimension that Dvořák handles without a shred of jingoistic nationalism.

Finally, there is the eternal conflict between the generations—between young and old in a time of social change—and an eloquent plea for understanding, forgiveness, and human decency. You should come out of *The Jacobin* feeling better about the world than when you went in. The music has a life-enhancing freshness unlike that of any other opera, which is perfectly captured in the lovely serenade that begins the second act (CD 1, track 9). This is a *set piece:* a stylized rehearsal of a homage cantata (the words aren't important) composed by the local schoolmaster, Benda, in honor of the return of Count Vilém to his ancestral home—abandoned since the death of his wife and banishment of his only son. The main theme of the children's choir will return at the opera's end, contrapuntally combined with the final chorus in one of the most joyous conclusions that Dvořák (no slouch in the joy department) ever penned.

The opening of the opera is pure comedy. As the villagers sing the final Sunday hymn and leave church, the schoolmaster Benda's daughter Terinka catches the eye of Filip, Count Vilém's governor. He is rich, old, pompous, and a lousy dancer. Benda thinks he would be a very advantageous match and behaves obsequiously to him, as befits a villager of the lower classes. The young folk, however, led by Terinka's boyfriend Jiří, ridicule Filip mercilessly until he slinks off. Meanwhile Bohuš, the count's estranged son, and his wife Julie arrive disguised as artists. They are refugees from Paris fleeing the French Revolution. Originally Bohuš had been attracted by the revolutionary ideals of freedom and equality, and this political dispute, fortified by the lies of his nasty cousin Adolf, caused the break with his father. Horrified by the behavior of the Jacobin regime, Bohuš was ultimately condemned to death as a counterrevolutionary, but his wife secured forged papers, and the two have escaped. Bohuš sings of his joy at being home at last and seeks a reconciliation with his embittered father.

At that very moment, the count arrives and announces that he has made Adolf his heir. Bohuš is naturally dismayed but does not approach his father. After the choir rehearsal, he visits Benda, asking for a place to stay. At first Benda refuses, but when he and Julie sing of their lonely wanderings in foreign lands, he relents. Terinka and Jiří's love is also developing at the same time. She sings a beautiful aria that turns into an enchanting love duet. Jiří is furious at the governor's attentions, and Terinka begs him to stop being so hotheaded. Benda cannot understand why his daughter refuses to even consider such a socially advantageous match and tells Jiři not to get his hopes up. Filip returns, Adolf in tow, and attempts to get Jiří drafted so as to have Terinka for himself. Bohuš confronts Adolf and demands to see his father. The revelation of his true identity shocks everyone, but Adolf has him arrested as a Jacobin sympathizer and later nabs Jiří as well.

Benda and Julie, meanwhile, gain access to the count. Julie hides while Benda attempts to ascertain the count's feelings towards his son, but the angry old man will not consider forgiveness. Benda leaves sadly, but Julie, seeing a portrait of the dead countess, has an idea. She accompanies herself on the harp in a lullaby that Bohuš taught her, exactly as his mother used to sing it. The count, deeply moved, looks for the source of the singing and finds Julie. She introduces herself as his daughter-in-law and, in a passionate exchange, reveals the truth about Bohuš's life in France, his escape from the Jacobins, and his imprisonment by Adolf. She demands justice for her husband. Furious at both himself and Adolf, the count accompanies Julie to Adolf's formal investment ceremony, where he demands, prior to turning over his titles, the right of pardoning any prisoners currently held in the castle jail. Bohuš is brought before him, and as the two reconcile, Benda blesses the union of Terinka and Jiří as well. The opera ends with festive singing and dancing.

In *The Jacobin*, Dvořák found a way to put an authentic Czech village setting to use in the service of a story that has universal relevance, and nothing at all in common with *The Bartered Bride*. He worked very closely with his librettist in fashioning the opera to his exact specifications, both for the original production and also for the revised version, which is the only form in which the opera is known today. Always a success in Prague, where it remains a repertory staple, it deserves a much wider audience. Music lovers the world over would surely respond to its warmth of feeling and wealth of realistic characterization, and to the special sweetness of music that never turns sentimental or maudlin. Above all, the music of *The Jacobin* is humane—and a worthy portrait, not just of the figures on stage, but of Dvořák himself.

The Devil and Kate

This wonderful, funny, fat-free comic opera deserves to rank with *Hansel and Gretel* in popularity. It's ideal for kids, and the only frightening thing about it is how well written it is. I have already discussed its bewitching stylistic blend of everything Dvořák knew, from Wagner to Offenbach, so I will limit this discussion to a brief synopsis of the plot and the strongest possible recommendation to hear the work for yourself. Actually, the story begins before the curtain rises. One of the criticisms sometimes leveled at this opera is that while the villagers speak of the evil Princess that they all hate, the audience doesn't actually get to see her until act 3, when she is frightened of the fate in store for her and repentant (if quite movingly so).

Aside from the obvious answer that this is a fairy tale, and any opera with a second act that takes place in hell isn't exactly concerned with true-to-life realism, Dvořák has in fact arranged that the audience see, or rather hear—both of the Princess and the unhappiness that she causes before she actually appears. Each of the acts takes place in a different realm: the village, hell, and the Princess's castle, and each of these has its own group of themes that also represent the three most important characters from each realm: the shepherd Jirka, the devil Marbuel, and the Princess. The overture, which functions more like one of the narrative symphonic poems described in chapter 6, begins with the theme of the Princess and continues in a tense, sometimes even tragic, vein. It perfectly describes her, the misery of her subjects, and the point at which she comes to the attention of the devil.

At its very end, the arrival of Jirka's theme signals the happy conclusion, but up until the last minute, the overture stays pretty much in gloomy minor keys. Dvořák has thus perfectly solved the problem of describing the character of the Princess and the people's suffering without resorting to lengthy plot digressions or, even worse, some perfunctory scene of gratuitous nastiness merely to make the point that she's as bad as the villagers say she is. The music does it all up front, and you don't even have to know anything about what the themes represent in advance of actually hearing them for the first time. You get all the information that you need simply by taking the music of the overture at face value, in the order in which Dvořák presents it.

Act 1 takes place in a village tavern. People are sitting around, drinking and grousing about the evil Princess and her miserable Steward. Jirka goes off to work, and Kate arrives. She's loud, coarse, and unattractive, and she complains that she can't find a partner despite the fact that she loves to dance. The devil Marbuel arrives looking for the steward to take him off to hell. Hearing Kate grouse, he offers to dance with her. Jirka returns, bitterly lamenting that he has been fired by the Steward for defending himself from a beating. At the same time, the devil, finding Kate to be obnoxious and mercenary enough to warrant his attention, describes to her the wealth of his castle—to the extremely remarkable instrumental accompaniment of two harps, two tubas, tam-tam, and contrabass clarinet, among other things. He invites her to join him there, and Kate agrees. The floor opens and Marbuel carries her off to hell. Jirka, who has no job anyway and nothing better to do, agrees to go after them and bring her back.

Meanwhile, down in hell, everyone is living it up à la Offenbach. Marbuel arrives with an extremely indignant Kate on his back. She has been berating him for deceiving her as to his true intentions. Lucifer orders Marbuel to return her, but Kate refuses to go until she's compensated for her trouble. Jirka arrives and suggests that the devil bribe her with some gold chains, and then pretends to show her a good time with some feasting and dancing. Everyone joins in a wild infernal dance (Dvořák's take on the famous "Can-Can" perhaps). Kate has a terrific time, and with her pockets stuffed with gold, she allows Jirka to dance her back through the gates of hell, to the relief of Marbuel, who now must go and get the Princess as planned (after agreeing with

Jirka to scare the Steward witless and into a permanent debt of gratitude).

In act 3, the Princess sings an absolutely stunning "repentance aria," not all that far in mood from (although less fearful than) Xenia's big number in the fourth act of *Dimitrij* (CD 1, track 8). She sends for Jirka, knowing that he saved the Steward and so perhaps can also save her from the fate that she admits she has earned. He agrees, on the condition that the Princess free the serfs and mend her ways. When she consents, Jirka reveals his secret plan in the form of Kate, who is mightily pissed that her gold turned to dead leaves as soon as she left hell. She wants to teach the devil a lesson he'll never forget. Hiding Kate behind a doorway as it becomes dark, Jirka waits for Marbuel, who arrives on schedule. As the Princess cowers before him, Jirka runs in and advises him to flee for his life; Kate obligingly steps out of hiding at the proper moment, and the terrified devil flies out the window. The Princess is saved, the serfs are free, and Kate gets lots of money and a big house.

So there you have it: a terrifically entertaining story, incredible music, and it's all over in about two hours. There's no more immediately appealing and well-crafted comic opera in the second half of the nineteenth century. If *The Devil and Kate* hasn't yet earned the respect of Wagner's or Verdi's contribution to the genre, it's certainly both different enough and good enough to withstand the comparison and take its place beside them.

Rusalka

Whether she's called Ondine, Undine, Lorelei, or the Little Mermaid, some variant of the *Rusalka* story survives in the legends of most countries. A few of these even became operas, the most famous prior example being Albert Lortzing's *Undine*, which

Dvořák must have known (he didn't play it at the Provisional Theater, but the company did perform three other Lortzing operas, and it would have been standard fare at the German opera house). The very familiarity of the story may be the factor most instrumental in making this Dvořák's most popular opera internationally. For that reason, there's little need to go into the minute details of the plot. Rusalka is a water spirit who falls in love with a mortal man (the Prince) whom she has seen coming to her lake. With the help of an obliging witch, she becomes a human so that she can live with him, but there's a catch: she is not permitted to speak, and should he leave her, she must return to her lake and claim his life when he comes to her, irresistibly drawn to the scene of their first meeting. We all know what happens next.

The most famous aria in the opera is Rusalka's popular "Song to the Moon" (CD 1, track 10), in which she pours out her innermost heart in a magnificently sustained river of melody. It became especially well known as a result of its use in the hit film *Driving Miss Daisy*, and by now it should be clear that the ravishing orchestration, memorable tune, and enchanting mood-setting is not unique in Dvořák but rather characteristic of him. Perhaps the most remarkable thing about *Rusalka* is the humanity with which Dvořák imbues these fantastic characters, especially the sympathetic "dirty old man" of a water sprite and the cranky witch. He's so good at it, in fact, that it strains credulity to hear his critics contend that he was unable to do the same for the actual people in his earlier operas. Rusalka herself is Dvořák's Aida, often displaying a similar combination of vulnerability and resolve.

Rusalka is also often cited as an example of Dvořák's having been influenced by Wagner, given the clear use of leitmotifs and the work's symphonic continuity. In the opening scene, the inspiration is obvious and—as in *The Devil and Kate*'s second act—

more than a little humorous. Wagner's *Das Rheingold* begins with three Rhine Maidens (water creatures) taunting a land creature (Alberich the dwarf). *Rusalka* begins with that scene's mirror opposite: three wood nymphs taunting the old water sprite. The parallelism is surely intentional, and quite amusing if you know your Wagner. As to the purely musical aspect, Wagner didn't invent leitmotifs, and Dvořák's mastery of musical continuity has nothing to do with him. Any composer as fine a symphonist and variation writer as he indisputably was, with as systematic a use of leitmotifs as, say, Puccini achieved in *Tosca* (written at the same time), could have arrived at something structurally akin to *Rusalka* had Wagner never existed.

Armida

Dvořák's last opera flopped at its premiere in 1904. Apparently it was badly performed, and the composer died suddenly, before he had a chance to make revisions (or not). Some commentators have expressed surprise that Dvořák chose such a shop-worn story, one set (as either *Armida* or *Orlando*, depending on the perspective) by such respected names as Handel, Gluck, Haydn, and Rossini, to name only the best known. In fact, it wasn't a bad move at all: the story of *Rusalka* was equally well known, both in its original form and as an opera, and the universality of the plot might easily have eased the opera's way into the international repertoire, as in fact has happened with its predecessor.

Indeed, looking at the text that Dvořák actually set, it's clear his take on the story is more original than that of any of his predecessors. Consider the basic story as derived from the Italian epic poet Tasso (more or less): Armida is a sorceress who falls in love with Roland, a knight on a crusade. She employs her magic arts to ensnare him, but with a little help from his friends and a handy magic shield, Roland gets rescued, and when he comes to his senses, he abandons her. She swears vengeance and rides off, Medea-like, in her chariot drawn by dragons. In some operatic versions, Roland leaves her with an apology and a promise to come back and visit when he's done crusading. There are various subsidiary characters and subplots, but this gives you the general picture.

In Dvořák's opera, Armida refuses to use her sex appeal to subvert the crusaders and save Damascus until she magically espies Roland in their camp. She has seen him in a dream and is already in love with him, as he is with her for the same reason. The evil magician in this opera is the king's adviser, Ismen, who secretly loves Armida as well. He wants to destroy Roland, but Armida uses her magical skills to protect him, and her confrontation with Ismen at the end of act 3 is one of the high points of the opera. Also, contrary to the other operas on the same subject, Roland's friends do not use their magic shield to break Armida's enchantment. It is a tool given to them by Ismen to enchant Roland *away* from her.

So in other words, Dvořák takes the position that the mysterious love that Armida and Roland feel for each other is what is real and true, while both pagan magic and Christian prayer-magic are effectively the same: evil forces attempting to keep the lovers apart. In the last act, as Roland successfully fights the Syrians and kills Ismen, Armida appears in armor and challenges him to battle. When she asks if he desires news of her, Roland says, in effect, that he wouldn't care if she were dead. At these words, Armida lowers her sword, and he runs her through (the idea for the scene comes from a different episode in Tasso: the battle between Trancred and Clorinda). Realizing what he has done breaks the enchantment that had taken hold of him, and as a regretful Roland baptizes the dying Armida, she dies in a state of grace. The final scene—in which the uncaring, victorious crusaders parade past Roland and the dead Armida—reveals a degree of tragic irony new to Dvořák's expressive arsenal.

Some critics have complained that the opera relies too heavily on Wagner, particularly the male choruses and the scenes in the crusaders' camp. This is silly. Crusaders invariably march around singing familiar-sounding hymns and religious chorales no matter what opera they turn up in. If Dvořák's crusaders sound like Wagner's *Tannhäuser* pilgrims, it's because the similarity makes dramatic sense, and both composers are making use of musical common coin in these and other such situations. Besides, Dvořák was trained as a church organist. If anyone knew how to write an effective hymn, Wagnerian or not, he did. *Armida* may not be Dvořák's most successful opera, but judgment as to its ultimate merits will not be possible absent an appreciation of his operatic achievement as a whole. Certainly the music is alternately powerful and beautiful, the orchestration imaginative, and the dramatic architecture confident. It's a good listen and, I suspect, a good evening of theater in a sympathetic production.

Perhaps the biggest difficulty in coming to grips with Dvořák's operatic achievement stems from the fact that there is no "typical" Dvořák opera. It is difficult to make many demonstrably valid assumptions about his theoretical conception of the medium as whole. I strongly doubt that he even had one, and frankly, that was no disadvantage for an artist in his unique position as the founder of a national school of musical expression, intent on exploring the range of possibilities open to him rather than defining a single "right way" forward.

That said, virtually all of his operas reveal a very strong egalitarian streak, particularly in their treatment of aristocratic characters, and this is so pronounced that it cannot be accidental.

The very title of *The King and the Charcoal Burner* speaks for itself in this respect. Vanda loves a commoner, Armida renounces her kingdom for love, and the prince in *Rusalka* pays the price of all mortals for his betrayal. The "bad guys" in *The Jacobin*, *The Cunning Peasant*, *Dimitrij*, and *The Devil and Kate* are all members of the nobility ultimately humbled by their social inferiors. Indeed, Dimitrij's stature as a tragic hero resides his willingness to die, having accepted the truth of his peasant birth.

The extent to which this observation can be related to any desire on Dvořák's part to project (whether overtly or covertly) certain political or patriotic beliefs is an open question, and care must be taken not to push the point too far. In considering his plot selections and treatments, a firmer case can be made for his evident desire to affirm the basic moral values of decency and shared humanity regardless of class. This is entirely consistent with Dvořák's belief in the universal appeal of music generally, extending beyond narrow national or cultural borders. However, it is quite different from the Wagnerian notion, often taken as a matter of course, that most composers have a consistent, preconceived theory of operatic dramaturgy that can be described in nonmusical terms. Some composers do, and others do not.

Dvořák was not that kind of musician. He was never a theorist. The composer he most resembles is Verdi, who wrote operas in a similarly wide mix of styles and genres over his long career, and like Verdi, it's easy to imagine Dvořák saying to his critics, "I may not be a learned composer, but I am a very experienced one." The comparison founders, however, on the fact that Verdi, despite his originality and variety, worked within a long, well-established national tradition. He is easy to place, both musically and historically. This is also true of Wagner. Dvořák, on the other hand, was unconstrained by any prior theories or schools of operatic thought, because everything he did for Czech music was new. He was a true pioneer in his own country but inevitably an eclectic traditionalist everywhere else, and therein lies the basic problem. Still, at the end of the day, it's musical quality that counts. I have no doubt whatsoever that Dvořák's operatic successes outnumber his failures, and that time is on his side.

Chamber Works

Of the three great composers of chamber music in the second half of the nineteenth century—Brahms, Dvořák, and the Frenchman Gabriel Fauré—Dvořák's contribution to the repertoire was the largest and arguably the finest. As a composer of string quartets in the 1800s, he is matched only by Beethoven, and Dvořák created masterpieces in every other medium in which he worked. It is here, appropriately, where Dvořák's profound love of the classical tradition reveals itself most tellingly. Except for an early clarinet quintet that was either lost or destroyed, he restricted himself to string ensembles or strings with keyboard. There are no works including wind or brass instruments (although Dvořák did write several pieces for combinations found nowhere else).

The sheer amount of music in this category makes extensive discussion of individual works impossible within the scope of this book. Happily, the various pieces fall relatively neatly into five large categories, the constituents of which have enough in common to make possible general descriptions, with reference to specific examples. You can then pursue your own interests in greater depth. This survey includes all the large-scale works for various chamber ensembles, as well as five major piano pieces—some twenty hours of music in all (covering some thirty-seven individual titles). As with the operas and the symphonies, not all of it is equally good, but the majority of this repertoire stands with the best in the genre and promises a lifetime of enjoyment.

Early Works

String Quintet No. 1 in A Minor, Op. 1 (1861)
Piano Quintet No. 1 in A, Op. 5 (1872)
String Quartet No. 1 in A, Op. 2 (1862)
String Quartet No. 2 in B-flat (1870)
String Quartet No. 3 in D (1870)
String Quartet No. 4 in E Minor (1870)
Silhouettes, Op. 8, for piano (1879)

Like that of the symphonies and operas, the origin of Dvořák's chamber music style has been the subject of much confusion. Only the first three of the above seven works, plus the piano cycle *Silhouettes*, survived with the composer's knowledge. String Quartets Nos. 2 through 4 he believed lost or destroyed, but parts turned up after his death and so allowed them to be rescued. If you come across any of these pieces and see commentators attribute some of their more unusual qualities (the use of chromatic harmony, three-movement forms, or single-movement, multisectional forms) to the "modern school" of Liszt and Wagner—which often happens—don't believe it.

Chamber music has always enjoyed greater structural and stylistic freedom than orchestral music, for the simple reason that in writing for smaller ensembles, the composer faces fewer performance problems and has greater latitude for experiment. Limitations in tone color and volume, when compared with the orchestra, can be overcome through a wider range of contrast achieved by means of harmony, form, and rhythm. Just like many of Dvořák's early chamber works, Mozart's piano quartets only have three movements each, as do most of Beethoven's violin sonatas and such later compositions as Brahms's String Quintet Op. 88. Both Schubert and Schumann experimented with multi-sectional pieces for both small and large forces that merge a conventional four-movement scheme into a single continuous whole (Schumann's Fourth Symphony and Schubert's *Wanderer Fantasy*, for piano, are particularly important in this regard).

In his late quartets, Beethoven adheres to no fixed formal scheme at all, finding a unique solution for each work. The nineteenth century in general was a fount of adventure in the chamber-music field. Some composers, quite successful or well known in their day, such as Berwald or Spohr, are hardly performed or remembered in our own time, although both were highly experimental in matters of structure and harmony. As a professional violist, Dvořák would have gained experience playing innumerable chamber works, both the great and the forgotten. Tracking down what he actually knew and what might have influenced the styles (for there are several) of these early pieces, even if possible, would require a lifetime of detective work and even then remain mostly speculation.

Nowhere is this more true than in the sphere of harmony. Just as in the classical period virtually every chromatic twist and turn gets attributed to Mozart, so in the romantic period it all comes to rest at Wagner's door. This is particularly foolish in considering chamber music. *Chromatic harmony* means melodies and chords that use notes foreign to the home key, undermining tonal stability—and this generally means emotional stability as well. When used properly, chromaticism heightens (or "colors," as the term implies) the music's expressive intensity, making it sound more poignant, dissonant, mysterious, sensual, or frightening. It can also lead to complete atonality (and many very unhappy listeners) when employed exclusively or to excess.

Arguably the single most chromatic piece of music in the entire nineteenth century is the finale of Chopin's Second Piano Sonata, and Spohr (1784–1859), who was the most famous living composer in Germany for quite a while, was using heavily chromatic harmony well before Wagner. Indeed, the fact that there is nothing comparable in Dvořák's early symphonies as compared, say, to those of Bruckner, strongly suggests that Dvořák's extensive use of chromaticism was a liberty he saw as valid primarily within the chamber-music tradition. Certainly the three "experimental" quartets, Nos. 2 through 4, reveal if anything a young composer's fascinating take, not on Wagner, but on the extended size, formal originality, and harmonic richness of late Beethoven, with perhaps a twist of Spohr thrown in for good measure.

The Second Quartet, at nearly forty minutes long, is a large work, full of memorable ideas developed more as a process of evolving variation (like many of the later slow movements) than according to the traditional rules of form. I suppose it does tend to ramble a bit, but it also flows along spontaneously, with surprisingly few dead spots. The opening of the largo sounds like a sketch for the first bars of the Sixth Symphony's slow movement. The Third Quartet is (I think) the longest such work ever composed in an ostensibly four-movement classical style. With all of its repeats, it plays for about seventy minutes, making it suited only to the most hard-core of Dvořákian true believers. If you purchase a complete set of all the quartets and have a lot of extra time on your hands, you may want to give it a spin. Otherwise, feel free to pass without feeling the least bit guilty.

The single-movement Fourth Quartet, with its relentless chromatic writing and busy counterpoint, often sounds like a peculiar Czech take on Beethoven's still shockingly modern *Grosse Fuge*. Even in this overwritten, extravagant, and lovably outrageous piece, Dvořák the melodist shines through. The central andante religioso ultimately became the haunting

Nocturne, Op. 40, for strings, and it offers a remarkable cross between the cavatina of Beethoven's Thirteenth Quartet and the melodic style of later composers such as Rachmaninov and Elgar (Dvořák brought the nocturne to England in 1884 for his first concerts there). Its melody returns very movingly just before the quartet's end.

The First Quartet and First Quintet really shouldn't be as good as they are given their early date, notwithstanding the fact that they were revised much later. The Quartet, in particular, makes a very fine impression and deserves to be heard more often. Its opening idea returns at the end of the finale in cyclical manner to round off the piece. The slow movement has a welcome degree of spontaneous passion, and the quiet ending of both outer movements recalls the often charming inspirations of Haydn and Mozart. In the String Quintet, which has three movements rather than four, Dvořák reveals a touching melancholy, admirably sustained, and its finale borrows a melody from the central lento. Piano Quintet No. 1 brings the composer to the verge of maturity. Its overall form (three movements again) has much in common—especially in the combination scherzo/finale—with the Third Symphony.

Dvořák was a good pianist, but his interest in the instrument was limited. He wrote about five hours' worth of solo keyboard music, mostly dances or suites of short character pieces of the type pioneered by Schumann. Seldom difficult or virtuosic, they nonetheless contain plenty of attractive music. The twelve *Silhouettes* are particularly interesting because they recycle many of the main themes from the first two symphonies, although always in varied form. In *Silhouette No. 6*, for example, the vivacious finale of the Second Symphony becomes a dreamy reverie at a much slower tempo. The following table lists the tunes from each symphony that appear in the various movements of the piano work. Comparing the two really is fun if you have the time and enjoy a bit of musical detective work now and then.

Silhouette No.	=	Symphony No.	Movement
1	=	1	1
5	=	1	1
6	=	2	4
8	=	1	3
9	=	1	4
11	=	2	3
12	=	1	1

The Classical Tradition

String Quartet No. 5 in F Minor, Op. 9 (1873)
String Quartet No. 6 in A Minor, Op. 12 (1873)
String Quartet No. 7 in A Minor, Op. 16 (1874)
String Quartet No. 8 in E Major, Op. 80 (1876)
String Quartet No. 9 in D Minor, Op. 34 (1877)
String Quartet No. 11 in C Major, Op. 61 (1881)
String Quartet No. 13 in G Major, Op. 106 (1895)
String Quartet No. 14 in A-flat Major, Op. 105 (1895)
Piano Quartet No. 1 in D Major, Op. 23 (1874)
Piano Quartet No. 2 in E -flat Major, Op. 87 (1889)
Piano Trio No. 1 in B-flat, Op. 21 (1875)
Piano Trio No. 2 in G Minor, Op. 26 (1876)
Piano Trio No. 3 in F Minor, Op. 65 (1883)
Violin Sonata in F, Op. 57 (1880)
Theme and Variations, Op. 36, for solo piano (1876)

With only three exceptions (the Theme and Variations, for solo piano; the First Piano Quartet; and the Violin Sonata), all the pieces here adopt full-scale, four-movement form, evidence of Dvořák's devotion to clear-cut, boldly articulated structures and his desire to write chamber music on the largest canvas. Like the Fourth Quartet, the Fifth yielded an independent work: the Romance in F, for violin and orchestra, but from the very beginning, Dvořák's personal melodic style is firmly in place. Like Schubert, he retained a fondness for tunes that slip back and forth from major to minor modes, and also for surprising key changes, harmonic excursions, and digressions, but the experimental chromaticism of Quartets 2 through 4 is largely gone for good.

The Sixth Quartet was never revised to Dvořák's satisfaction. Originally a single span having four linked sections (like Schumann's Fourth Symphony), he intended to break it up into four distinct movements but never finished the job. What remains today is a skillful conceptual realization based on Dvořák's pretty clear intentions, but the work can't be said to represent his final thoughts. From the Seventh Quartet on, though, it's smooth sailing, and along with the First and Fourth Quartets, this makes ten pieces that display the composer's stylistic progress and increasing formal mastery of this most difficult medium over a period of more than three decades. No other composer of the period devoted so much time and effort to the string quartet or succeeded to such a degree.

All the remaining works are worth hearing, and the list on page 102 contains only those quartets that have no particular relationship with other important stylistic trends in Dvořák's music. Those you will find further on in this chapter. This batch belongs to what you might call "the absolute of the absolute," music that has no obvious recourse to ethnic elements or local color, but sits comfortably in the great Central European tradition initiated by Haydn. The Ninth Quartet was humbly dedicated to Brahms. The Eleventh Quartet, which was intended for a Vienna premiere, displays the composer's Schubertian credentials most vividly—

and it has to be said, politically correctly given the times—in Schubert's favorite key of C major.

In 1895, after his final return from New York, Dvořák sat down and wrote his last two quartets, widely regarded as comparable in musical mastery and individuality to the late efforts of Beethoven. It's difficult not to hear in this music a joyful farewell to the Viennese classical tradition. The remainder of Dvořák's career would be occupied with the late symphonic poems and with opera. The craftsmanship, motivic work, and formal control bring to mind Haydn and Mozart as well, but the tunes could only have come from Dvořák, as you can hear for yourself on CD 1, track 11, where you will find the first movement of Quartet No. 14, Op. 105.

The movement begins with a slow introduction presenting a simple melodic figure with a characteristic turn. This becomes the principal idea of the first subject group (at 1:13), ending with one of those typical three-note motives that have a tendency to detach themselves and take on an independent existence. Further ideas include a singing transition theme (or *cantabile*, at 1:29) over a *pizzicato* (plucked) bass in the cello, and a rhythmic motive in the minor (1:45) beginning with another three-note figure—you can't miss it. The second subject is a catchy tune in "hunting" rhythm (2:27).

There is no exposition repeat. The development section begins with a reference to the opening adagio (3:08), proceeds directly to the first subject, introduces the second in the cello (3:53), and combines them both (4:08) in vigorous exchanges among all four players. A variant of the cantabile theme (4:52) leads to an altered version of the three-note motive from the end of the first subject (5:10) and slyly initiates the recapitulation (at 5:22). Dvořák shortens the reprise of the first subject drastically, leaving out the cantabile and cutting quickly to the second subject (5:57).

A final, expanded return to the slow introduction (6:39) leads to an accelerating close based on the first subject.

Even though these works do not use obvious Czech or nationalistic elements, they are in no way deficient in those beautiful, characteristic melodies that listeners expect from Dvořák. This is especially true of the piano trios, another medium in which his achievement is perhaps equaled only by Beethoven (although Brahms was also impressive in this department). The Third Trio, in F minor, is often compared to the Seventh Symphony as a sort of apotheosis of Dvořák's work in the classical style, and with good reason. Although the work has four movements, the scherzo, with its delightful simultaneous clash of duple and triple rhythms, comes second—not unusual considering chamber music's often greater formal freedom as compared to symphonic writing.

However, rather than making a point of this trio's perfection of form, I want to draw your attention instead to the gorgeous tunes of its slow movement (CD 2, track 1). There are four of them, arranged almost like a free improvisation in this order: ABACDBA–coda (DB). Section A is a slow meditation initially for the cello, in three phrases that open out like a blooming flower. B (1:04) has a slightly quicker rhythm and always features at least two instruments (initially violin and cello) in close imitation. After a more lyrically expansive return of A (2:00), Dvořák offers a violent contrast in the form of C (3:39), a jagged tune initiated by the piano hauntingly mixing major and minor modes, answered by D (4:18), the most ecstatically lyrical episode in the entire movement.

The return to B, initially, permits the tranquil beauty of A (6:44) to bring the main body of the movement to a close without undue repetition, but the players seem unwilling to let the vision of peace go, and so Dvořák provides a nostalgic coda (8:29) in which D and B reappear like memories, all passion spent. Formally this movement is a type of rondo, but honestly, does it matter? To anyone reasonably knowledgeable, the identity of the composer would be clear in about ten seconds. The music has that much sheer strength of melodic personality, an intrinsic artistic quality that can never be taught.

The two piano quartets are also fine works, the first a three-movement piece that, like the First Piano Quintet, reveals a certain kinship with the contemporaneous Third Symphony. Its last movement, like that of the symphony, combines the functions of a finale with the lightness of a scherzo, while the middle movement is a beautiful theme and variations that once again reveals Dvořák's mastery of this particular form. The Second Piano Quartet dates from the same period as the Eighth Symphony, which means it stands at the very apex of Dvořák's melodic individuality. It has always been extremely popular, as well as frequently recorded, and it never fails to please both players and listeners alike. Remarkably for a chamber work, it reveals an uncommon preoccupation with instrumental color, and it offers some especially ear-catching piano sonorities in its gracious third movement.

This brief survey of Dvořák's more classical-style chamber music concludes with two singleton works. The sunny Violin Sonata (in three movements, like many of Mozart's and Beethoven's) shares the same key and lyrical freshness as the Violin Concerto, and it was composed at about the same time, when Dvořák was making his first major revision of the orchestral work. The finales of both owe a debt to Czech dance elements, even though they don't specifically say so. The Theme and Variations, for solo piano—Dvořák's largest single movement for the instrument—aside from being a marvelous essay in variation form also has an orchestral partner: the Symphonic Variations, which date from a couple of years later. It deserves more exposure on concert programs than it currently receives, largely because many concert pianists don't even know that it exists.

Slavonic Works

String Sextet in A, Op. 48 (1878)
Piano Quintet No. 2 in A, Op. 81 (1887)
String Quartet No. 10 in E Flat, Op. 51 ("Slavonic") (1879)
Piano Trio No. 4 , Op. 90 ("Dumky") (1891)
Terzetto in C, Op. 74, for two violins and viola (1887)
From the Bohemian Forest, Op. 68, for piano duet (1884)

Given Dvořák's reputation as *the* founder of the Czech national school in all genres except opera, it may surprise you just how few overtly nationalist pieces he wrote. Essentially, this trait consists of replacing the traditional scherzo or slow movement with a Czech dance, either a *furiant* (a quick piece with clashing duple and triple rhythms), or a *dumka*, which is actually Ukrainian in origin and which in Dvořák's hands became a rhapsodic piece in which slow, sad sections alternate with passages expressing wild, high spirits.

Since the vast majority of his work in general reflects the influence of Czech folk music and dance rhythms whether he explicitly says so or not, Dvořák generally preferred to let these elements speak for themselves, so as not to encourage nationalistic prejudice and limit his appeal. However, in this particular group of pieces, as in the Fifth and Sixth Symphonies with their furiant scherzos, he made the ethnic flavor particularly explicit. This is what most people historically expect from a "nationalistic" composer, and these works accordingly number among his most popular, without necessarily being better than the others.

The String Sextet has a dumka second movement and a furiant for its third. You can hear the latter on CD 1, track 12. This movement (at 01:33) shares a tune with the first of the Slavonic Dances. By general consent, however, the Sextet's most imaginative part is the finale, which is another theme and variations. It's typical of Dvořák's wider project of integrating nationalist elements into the musical mainstream that he follows the two central movements with a finale in a deliberately learned, more obviously intellectual style. It's also a very classical thing to do in terms of the work's larger balance and symmetry. The Second Piano Quintet, which begins with a luscious opening tune on the cello, also has the same order of inner movements as the Sextet. Its dumka is the largest and most elaborate that Dvořák ever wrote, and it expresses truly profound sadness. The furiant is of a type similar to the scherzo of the Fifth Symphony, and its middle (trio) section consists simply of the main tune slowed down.

The Terzetto, for two violins and viola—an inventive work for its unusual combination of instruments (the standard string trio has one each of violin, viola, and cello)—also sports a furiant scherzo, prefacing, as in the sextet, a brilliantly inventive theme-and-variations finale. The Tenth String Quartet has a dumka for its second movement, but the whole work seems particularly Slavic in expression, hence the nickname. However, the famous "Dumky" Trio, with its six dance movements in a row (*dumky* is the plural of *dumka*), is not only a landmark in using nationalist elements to create a large work with no trace of classical forms, it's probably the single most popular and beloved piano trio ever written. It also represents the logical culmination of the process of formal experimentation begun in the Eighth Symphony of two years previously.

Dvořák wrote several fine pieces for piano duet, most of which (the two sets of Slavonic Dances and the *Legends*) he also orchestrated, and so will be considered in "Miscellaneous

Orchestral Works." *From the Bohemian Forest,* however, remains largely a piano duet, save for a single movement, "Silent Woods," later most beautifully arranged for cello and orchestra. Its colorful titles ("In the Spinning Room," "Witches' Sabbath," "In Troubled Times") were bound to appeal to domestic consumers of ethnic novelties, just as the music itself reveals Dvořák as a master in the field of light pieces for talented amateurs to play and enjoy at home. Dvořák's piano music, unjustly maligned though it is, almost always reveals a keen ear for keyboard color, and of course the tunes speak for themselves.

American Works (and Dvořák's American Period in General)

String Quintet No. 3 in E-flat, Op. 97 (1893)
String Quartet No. 12 in F Major, Op. 96 ("American") (1893)
Sonatina in G, Op. 100, for violin and piano (1893)
Humoresques, Op. 101, for piano (1894)

Everyone agrees that the works of Dvořák's American period sound a bit different from his other pieces, but there's a big question about just how "American" this sound truly is, where it came from, and what his intentions were in adopting it in the first place. It's surely no accident that the four works above were composed in the first flush of enthusiasm for the sounds of the New World—and in particular, Negro spirituals and Native American music—but there's more to it than that. In synthesizing these influences and producing melodies cast to some extent in their image, Dvořák also foreshadowed much of the noteworthy American popular music to come, particularly ragtime, jazz, and musical theater.

This is easier to hear than it is to describe, so I offer for your consideration the finale of <u>String Quartet No. 12,</u> the so-called "American" Quartet, on CD 2, track 3. Many of the themes in this quartet fall into categories that I've discussed before. The opening melody of the first movement, on the viola, is a question-and-answer tune. The scherzo begins with a mirror theme, first phrase up, second phrase down, and continues with Iowa birdsong (Dvořák said so). In the finale, despite the intimate chamber-music context, we encounter one of the composer's most evocative train tunes: you can almost imagine the sound of the locomotive that brought the Dvořák family to Spillville, Iowa in the summer of 1893, where he spent his evenings listening to Native American songs and dances and, in the space of a few days, jotted down this quartet.

The beginning of the finale is pure syncopated rhythm, among the most obvious characteristics of both ragtime and jazz, and also, incidentally, common to Czech folk music. This rhythmic introduction persists for several seconds before settling down into a chugging accompaniment on the second violin, viola, and cello (0:16). The main theme (0:22), like most of the melodies in this quartet, is largely pentatonic. In other words, it is based on a five-note scale similar to those found in Chinese music—and indeed, folk music the world over. This gives it a starkly primitive character, so much so that when Dvořák introduces some simple harmony in double-stops into its continuation (at 1:03), the effect is almost shockingly sensual. Through it all, Dvořák subtly varies the underlying patterns and accents as the movement proceeds, relaxing the pace now and then to provide a few moments of lyrical contrast.

Simple tunes over strongly rhythmic, often syncopated accompaniments are certainly characteristics of later American music, but in 1893 this meant the popular rather than the classical stuff, and it came from a race that most white people at the time would scarcely have acknowledged as truly "American" at all. Yet, you may feel in listening to this movement that the "Western" populist style of Aaron Copland isn't very far away, and you would be right. Indeed, three of the most important twentieth-century American composers—Copland, George Gershwin, and Duke Ellington—had a direct connection with Dvořák, through his students and fellow faculty at the National Conservatory in New York.

On CD 2, track 2, you will find the Humoresque No. 4, for piano, which takes the listener on a surprising harmonic adventure—in this case, an anticipation of 1950s lounge music. Its opening phrase with its bluesy harmony gets repeated four times, with slightly different chords and dynamics on each recurrence. It sounds improvised, or maybe a bit like Gershwin meeting French composer Francis Poulenc (the first of his *Mouvements perpétuels*), or even like that great iconoclast Eric Satie. The next episode (0:36) takes an almost insultingly childlike motive and spices it up harmonically four different ways, all within the space of a few seconds. The opening theme returns (1:10), twice repeated, at first more jazzy-sounding then ever and then comparatively "square," in simpler harmony.

The second episode (1:32) is the most remarkable of all. Stylistically it reeks of the music hall and such pieces as Joplin's *Pine Apple Rag* (1908). In fact, the tune is basically the same in outline as that old chestnut "Jeepers, Creepers," by Johnny Mercer and Harry Warren (1938). I am not suggesting that Warren borrowed from Dvořák. The point lies in the coincidence: paradoxically, Dvořák's American works often sound most original just when their thematic material is at its most commonplace. So is this episode American music? Not so fast! Compare it to the Slavonic Dance, Op. 72, No. 5; on CD 2, track 7, at 0:35. There you also find the same tune in its essentials, but it's as Czech as Czech can be. Finally, consider that Dvořák originally thought about calling the Humoresques "New Scottish Dances," noting certain tonal similarities between Scottish folk music and indigenous American tunes as well (he had already written a set of Scottish Dances, for piano, some years earlier).

The eight Humoresques are, in general, delicious little studies in harmony as applied to differently shaped fragments of popular melody. The Seventh Humoresque is probably the most famous small piano work ever written after Beethoven's *Für Elise*, and you can still hear it today in everything from television commercials to nursery school songs, as well as in jazz legend Art Tatum's celebrated improvisations. Those who find its unforgettable opening tune a bit corny should stick around and listen to what happens when it twice returns later on, and has a remarkable encounter with the end of the blues melody from the central section of Gershwin's *An American in Paris* (composed several decades later).

Perhaps the most American thing about this particular group of chamber pieces, then, is the resemblance of their thematic material to popular songs, and since American pop idioms effectively conquered the world in the twentieth century, it may also very well be that these Dvořák pieces have actually come to sound *more* "American" over time than they did when he wrote them and "Negro melodies" were treated as a thing apart from the musical mainstream. Certainly they are all audibly cut from shared cloth. The String Quintet's second movement begins with a syncopated rhythm similar to that of the Quartet's finale and proceeds to what amounts to a country hoedown. Its last movement features a tune from the same family as Humoresque No. 7. Even the charming Sonatina, which Dvořák wrote for his children (and also, in a humorous vein, to minimize the imposing significance of having reached his Op. 100), begins with a hymn-like melody that might have come from a revival meeting.

American popular song in the first decades of the twentieth century evolved out of a fusion of African American ragtime, early jazz, and the Eastern European Slavonic melos of immigrant Jewish composers. This was the school that produced Gershwin, Irving Berlin, Al Jolson, Jerome Kern, Benny Goodman, and others too numerous to name. It also describes the melodic style of Dvořák's American works quite well, even if, as an established classical composer, he mixes these ingredients a bit differently.

Dvořák's American period has come in for much recent scholarly scrutiny as a result of the increased respect paid to Golden Age jazz and American musical theater in the first half of the twentieth century, music that has effectively earned "classical" status in the way that great art always does: by withstanding that test of time. This makes his public declaration that African American and popular music idioms would ultimately serve as the basis of a new national school seem remarkably astute rather than merely eccentric, and the example he set in his own works marks him as a true cultural pioneer, perhaps even something of a visionary. Certainly this is the view of Maurice Peress in his very smart and refreshing book *Dvořák to Ellington: A Conductor Explores America's Music and Its African American Roots* (Oxford University Press, 2004). If this particular topic interests you further, I suggest that you start here.

One-of-a-Kind Novelties

String Quintet No. 2 in G, Op. 77 ("Double Bass") (1875)
Cypresses, for string quartet (1887)
Bagatelles, Op. 47, for string trio and harmonium (1878)
Romantic Pieces, Op. 75, for violin and piano (1887)
Poetic Tone Pictures, Op. 85, for piano (1889)

This grab bag of miscellaneous pieces contains some of Dvořák's most appealing music, as well as his greatest single piano work.

The other really significant item is the String Quintet No. 2, with double bass, an otherwise unheard of combination possibly inspired by Schubert's *Trout Quintet*, for piano and strings. The problem with the double bass within the context of the classical chamber-music style is that it lives in a fundamentally different timbral realm than all other stringed instruments, and the ear simply does not accept its presence as an equal partner in the ensemble. Knowing this full well, Dvořák makes a virtue out of necessity and creates a work rich in color and humor and tremendously varied in texture, as the double bass surfaces now and then like a sort of musical hippopotamus coming up from the bottom of a lake for air.

The slow movement of this quintet is exceptionally beautiful, even for Dvořák, with an ecstatic middle section that's unforgettably lyrical. Originally the work had an additional slow movement, placed second: none other than that andante religioso of the Fourth Quartet, now renamed "Nocturne," with a double bass part added. This was the penultimate stop for what finally became the independent Nocturne, Op. 40, for string orchestra. More to the point, the original five-movement structure highlights the relationship to the similarly organized Schubert *Trout Quintet* noted above and also gives a clue to the music's genial, serenade-like character.

Cypresses, for string quartet, grew out of one of Dvořák's earliest song collections, composed for his student and first great love, Josefina. Several of the songs were later revised and published as Op. 83, but unwilling to let the music go, Dvořák also arranged a dozen of them for strings. They are lovely, gentle, elegiac in feeling, and fine examples of his tuneful early style. The Bagatelles, for string trio and harmonium, occupy a special place in the hearts of all Dvořák lovers, for they crystallize the essence of his melodic purity and charm. You can hear the first movement on CD 2, track 4. The tune, part of which supposedly incorporates a fragment of a Czech folk song, strikingly anticipates the style of the later American works, doubtless a result of the music's directness and simplicity. Note the switch from minor to major as the melody proceeds—a classic Dvořák fingerprint.

The four Romantic Pieces exist in two versions, a well-known later one for violin and piano, and the original, under the title *Miniatures*, for two violins and viola (like the Terzetto). They were in fact written because the amateur players for whom Dvořák created the Terzetto found the music too difficult, but rather than let this attractive little cycle alone, he rearranged them once again. Their order is unusual: three relatively short and quick movements precede a much longer, slower, divinely songful conclusion that does indeed sound very romantic. They make great encore items at violin recitals.

Finally, *Poetic Tone Pictures* is Dvořák's largest piano cycle. He intended all thirteen movements, which collectively last about fifty minutes, to be played together, and he arranged them for maximum contrast accordingly. There are remarkable individual items here, ranging from the moody proto-impressionism of "At the Old Castle" (No. 3) to the grandeur of "At the Tomb of a Hero" (No. 12), which has a middle section of a strikingly Spanish character (almost like prophetic anticipation of Albeniz's *Iberia*). Most significantly, this work vividly represents Dvořák's increasing involvement with programmatic and illustrative music, which would occupy him extensively throughout the 1890s.

In concluding this survey of the chamber works, it's worth remembering two facts. First, despite the small size of the ensemble, the music itself operates on the same generous scale as the symphonies from a structural point of view. Second, even disregarding the ethnic elements, Dvořák was an inherently colorful composer. Pianists may carp at the layout of his keyboard parts, but they invariably sound imaginatively conceived in context. His string writing, furthermore, takes advantage of the full range of playing techniques—such as pizzicato, tremolo, double- and triple-stops, and bowing on the bridge of the instrument (*sul ponticello*)—and this gives the music its refreshing variety of texture. In short, Dvořák's chamber output does not make a fetish out of self-denial. On the contrary, it is rich in invention, warm in spirit, and as always, abundantly endowed with distinctive melody. Few things in art are more difficult than remaining both consistently interesting and strikingly beautiful. No one managed it better than Dvořák did in his chamber works.

Choral Music and Songs

The Heirs of the White Mountain (1872)
Moravian Duets (1875)
Stabat Mater (1877)
Gypsy Melodies (1880)
The Specter's Bride (1884)
St. Ludmila (1886)
Mass in D (1887)
Requiem (1890)
Te Deum (1892)
The American Flag (1893)
Biblical Songs (1894)

vořák, although best known for his instrumental music, wrote at least as large a body of vocal works. Aside from the operas and the above list of important compositions involving the human voice, there are over a hundred songs and a substantial body of smaller choruses, both accompanied and unaccompanied. The reasons that most of this music is not better known today are easy to pinpoint. First, the Czech works pose a language barrier, while the large oratorios suffer from the general neglect of all such nineteenth-century works designed to serve the British market, where Dvořák was without question the hottest foreign novelty in the 1880s and 90s. He visited England nine times, spoke and wrote the language, and did some of his finest work with English audiences in mind.

Obviously one's own affection for any musical genre will be a matter of personal taste, and big nineteenth-century English choral works, like French grand operas, happen to be terribly out of fashion today. This is a pity for English-speaking music lovers, because Latin works aside, all of Dvořák's large choral works were published with English (and German) texts, and so can be performed with little extra effort in the translation department. Of course the Victorian-style poetry is often dreadful, but really, so what? Either it's part of the period flavor of the whole thing or else it's a relatively simple matter to clean up the most obvious examples of mangled syntax and rhetorical excess. What matters is that the music is marvelous.

The Heirs of the White Mountain

The American Flag

These two works belong together because of both their patriotic content and the contrasts in the way that Dvořák set them. *The Heirs of the White Mountain* is a deeply felt, warm expression of patriotic sentiment for chorus and orchestra lasting a bit more than fifteen minutes. It has to be said that Dvořák was an excellent writer of hymnlike music, and this always serves a choral composer well. The text, which is no better or worse than most examples of its type, has been translated into English for singing purposes, and so the piece can be easily performed in countries speaking that language. The scoring, for a normal orchestra of double winds and standard brass, plus timpani, harp, and strings, poses no special problems. As always with Dvořák, the writing for the voices is richly sonorous, and he wrings an impressive amount of color out of the orchestra too, particularly the harp and wind sections. This piece won Dvořák his first big success as a composer, and no wonder. It's an accomplished piece of work, confident and without a trace of bombast.

The American Flag, on the other hand, was commissioned by Jeannette Thurber, patron of the National Conservatory. The militaristic poem (by Joseph Rodman Drake) is pretty bad: "Ere yet the life blood, warm and wet / Has dimm'd the glist'ning bayonet / Each soldier's eye shall brightly turn / To where thy sky born glories burn," etc. Although Dvořák told Mrs. Thurber that he thought the words very grand, he understandably put off setting them for as long as possible. If ever a composer was a musical pacifist, it was Dvořák. His operas do contain a couple of brief battle scenes, but one percussion instrument he hardly ever used was the snare drum, and even his *Festival March,* Op. 54 (1879), struts along amusingly in a syncopated rhythm to which no human being could ever really march.

It would be foolish to claim that he approached this work with any particular personal conviction, but as a thorough professional, he did a decent enough job, attacking that snare drum with a relish that makes it impossible not to suspect that he had a good bit of fun in the process. He also kept it short: the work's eight movements last barely twenty minutes. Even more interestingly, Dvořák knew better than to use this piece as a launching pad for his theory about African American music serving as the basis for a national musical culture. Since recognizably Czech coloring would be inappropriate as well, the results are amiable but more than a little anonymous. Dvořák's theoretical peasant naiveté has always been exaggerated. He was, in truth, an exceptionally astute musical politician, and like all good ones, he instinctively understood when to do the diplomatic thing and play it safe. Happily, he didn't have to do it often.

Moravian Duets

In 1875, the still little-known Dvořák was working as a music
teacher to the talented children of a patriotic Prague merchant
family headed by Mr. Jan Neff. Noting the absence of Czech
songs for vocal duet, Mr. Neff gave Dvořák some Moravian
verses and melodies, and asked him to arrange them for two
voices and piano. Dvořák, very significantly in terms of his later
musical development, kept the poems but scrapped the melodies,
substituting his own original tunes instead. They were a hit, and
when he applied for the Austrian State Grant in that same year,
he sent them off to the committee that included both Brahms and
the powerful critic Eduard Hanslick. Enchanted by the pieces,
Brahms turned them over to his publisher Fritz Simrock, who
bought them for a pittance, translated them into German, and
made a fortune selling them. Shortly thereafter, he commissioned
Dvořák to write the first set of eight Slavonic Dances, and the
rest, as they say, is history. Dvořák made two powerful friends,
had a publisher, and gained a worldwide audience.

Nowadays these charming miniatures are usually sung in
arrangements for chamber choir. There are three sets, published
as Opp. 20, 32, and 38 respectively, containing twenty-three
pieces in all. The Op. 20 set is arranged for soprano and tenor,
the other two for soprano and alto. The poems cover the usual
subjects: love gained and lost, and the joy of spring. Also,
significantly for Dvořák (who was a fanatical pigeon breeder),
birds figure prominently in many of them. Amateur choirs,
particularly of women or children, would find these little pieces
(most scarcely last two or three minutes) every bit as refreshing
and delightful as Brahms did. The only reason for their neglect in
English-speaking countries is the language barrier, and perhaps
also the fact that chorus directors don't necessarily think of them
as choral works in the first place.

Stabat Mater

The Stabat Mater is a very vivid and moving prayer that conjures up the image of the Virgin Mary grieving at the foot of the cross upon which Jesus has just died. In reciting the text, the supplicant asks to share the burden of the Holy Mother's grief and to experience the purifying pain of Christ's sacrifice, thus becoming worthy of the Virgin's intercession and access to paradise on the Day of Judgment. It is not a short poem, but at about eighty-five minutes, Dvořák's is incomparably the largest setting of it. The work arose out of the direst personal tragedy: within two years in the mid-1870s, the Dvořáks lost all three of their children, two to illness and one to accidental poisoning. Most biographers attempting to find links between Dvořák's music and his personal life are grasping at straws, but here the evidence is compelling.

The Stabat Mater, though certainly somber, is not in the least self-pitying or despairing. Dvořák was never, ever, a romantic artist in the stereotypical sense: a sorrowful, Byronic, brooding egomaniac filling his works with manic extremes of misery and elation. Berlioz, Tchaikovsky, and Wagner all fit that description to greater or lesser degree. Aside from being a deeply religious Catholic, Dvořák's solace was his music, and he catches the full meaning of the text, which is not to suffer for its own sake, but rather to empathize with the sorrow of Christ's mother as part of a process that leads ultimately to consolation and hope. Even though this is a long work, requiring great concentration in performance from both listeners and executants, its very sincerity and simplicity make it a profoundly touching experience, and it rightly enjoys a high reputation among choral music enthusiasts.

Part of the reason no doubt stems from the extremely intelligent way that Dvořák organizes the whole. The work opens with a chorus nearly a full twenty minutes long, perhaps the most impressively sustained choral lament since the opening

of Bach's *St. Matthew Passion*. Next comes a solo quartet about half
that length, and as the work proceeds, the movements in general
become progressively shorter. So it gets easier as it goes. Dvořák
also shows great variety in arranging his forces:

No. 1: Solo Quartet and Chorus
No. 2: Solo Quartet
No. 3: Chorus
No. 4: Bass Solo and Chorus
No. 5: Chorus
No. 6: Tenor Solo and Chorus
No. 7: Chorus
No. 8: Soprano and Tenor Duet
No. 9: Alto Solo
No. 10: Solo Quartet and Chorus

Notice how the use of solo voices moves from lower to higher,
from darkness to light, with the only true solo number, for alto,
coming next to last. Her aria, "Inflammatus et accensus," has a
strongly baroque flavor with its stalking bass lines and expressive
coloratura, although the exquisite orchestration and the melodies
are recognizably Dvořák. Both here and elsewhere in the work,
his unmistakably personal expression mingles with the ritual-
ized gestures of public prayer. This technique makes the piece a
curiously compelling mixture of familiar and original elements.
Some commentators have criticized the Stabat Mater (somewhat
generically) for this seeming stylistic patchwork, but it strikes
me, on the contrary, as Dvořák's way of making the prayer his
own while paying homage to the great tradition of sacred music
from which it comes.

The scoring, for double winds, standard brass (two trumpets,
four horns, three trombones and tuba), timpani, and strings,
with English horn and organ (or harmonium), also shows great

sensitivity in the accompaniments, with constantly shifting colors and a number of very expressive woodwind solos. The Stabat Mater was hugely popular (ironically enough) in its day, especially in England, where it led to Dvořák's fruitful ongoing association with that nation's concert life. Certainly not a work to be taken lightly, it poses few technical problems in performance (aside from the usual need to find four excellent soloists who work well as a team), while its emotional honesty and freedom from lachrymose sentimentality have preserved it as a repertory item, with new recordings appearing regularly as well.

Gypsy Melodies

Biblical Songs

Dvořák's songs are shamefully neglected, largely on account of their language. Most are simple in form, but they are often strikingly original in melody and harmony. More than a few reflect his great admiration and (for the period) extensive knowledge of Schubert. Despite the title, *Gypsy Melodies* contains no Gypsy melodies. As usual, all the tunes are original, if aptly Slavic/ Magyar/Romany in tone, and this set of seven songs includes Dvořák's most famous contribution to the form: "Songs My Mother Taught Me." This genuine "greatest hit" has been arranged numerous times as a purely instrumental number, particularly as a solo for violin or cello.

The idea for the ten *Biblical Songs* evidently came to Dvořák in 1894 following the death of two of his friends: the conductor Hans von Bulow and Tchaikovsky. Interestingly, it would seem that Dvořák had *only* friends: virtually everyone liked him, and few if any ever had a hostile thing to say about him personally.

(Bulow's death, as it turns out, was artistically stimulating in several respects, for it also provided the inspiration for the finale of Mahler's Second Symphony ["Resurrection."])

These moving songs, all based on Czech translations of the Psalms, have made a profound impression in their English versions, where they can still be heard in numerous Anglican/Protestant churches on any given Sunday ("The Lord Is My Shepherd" is understandably the most popular). Dvořák orchestrated the first five of them for an elegant chamber ensemble of pairs of flutes, clarinets, horns, and trumpets; with timpani, harp, triangle, and strings. The remaining songs were arranged for the same forces after the composer's death. They would grace any concert program.

One of the biggest problems with the classical song (or *Lieder*) repertoire is that almost all of them from Schubert on were actually written for amateurs to sing at home. Unfortunately, they are now usually performed by opera singers in an artificially inflated manner, in circumstances as stiff, uncomfortable, and inappropriately formal as the music is generally unpretentious and accessible. The reason for this, from the elitist perspective, is to distinguish them from popular songs, which differ from them in no particular way at all. A good song is a good song: the criteria for one (words that move the listener and a memorable musical setting) are the same no matter what.

The Specter's Bride

The Specter's Bride is a ghost story, and like all good ghost stories, it manages to be creepy, fun, and outrageous, all at the same time. Indeed, I can't think of any composer who so perfectly conjures up the musical equivalent of staying up late with your friends and spinning a good yarn to give them an amiable jolt. The story, which like *Rusalka* exists in the legends of many countries, tells the tale of a young girl pining for the return of her boyfriend, who unknown to her is already dead. In her frustration at his absence, she commits blasphemy: she prays to God for his return or else, she swears, she will kill herself. Sure enough, the boyfriend turns up and takes her on a wild, hellish chase through the countryside to his "home," which turns out to be a cemetery.

Tossing her wedding veil over the cemetery fence as a decoy, she barricades herself in the dead-house with an unburied corpse. When pounding on the door doesn't induce her to come out, her fiancé animates the corpse three times, each time forestalled by the girl's feverish prayers. In her third prayer, she pulls out all the stops in a heartfelt plea for divine assistance, and at that moment, dawn breaks and the evil spirits disperse. As the sun rises, the bloodied, exhausted girl is found in the dead-house, dazed but alive, her wedding veil shredded and draped over the branches of the trees in the cemetery. The moral of the story: be careful what you pray for—you may get it, and next time the good Lord may not be so merciful.

It's clear that Dvořák had a blast with this tale, creating a work that really has few parallels in the choral literature. The music plays continuously for about seventy-five minutes, and the various numbers (for chorus plus three characters: the soprano girl, the tenor ghost, and a baritone narrator) are tightly organized in three large spans—as carefully arranged as any symphony. Although there are nineteen numbers in all, the work takes the following basic form:

I

Introduction (orchestra)
Prayer (soprano)
Duet: (tenor and soprano)

II

The Flight to the Cemetery (three sequences of narrations and dialogues)

III

Cemetery Scene (three numbers)

Prayer (soprano)

Postlude (baritone and chorus)

Note the magic number three: like all the best ghost-story tellers, Dvořák understands the need for a symmetrical stretching out of the tale (as well as the listener's credulity). He's aided by a particularly skillful orchestration. The score requires two flutes plus piccolo; two oboes plus English horn; two clarinets plus bass clarinet; two bassoons, four horns, two trumpets, three trombones, tuba, timpani, harp, and strings. In the cemetery scene, Dvořák adds triangle and tam-tam, and the dawn sequence at the conclusion has an especially effective part for the glockenspiel. So as the work proceeds, he's constantly enriching the music's color—the more preposterous the story gets, the more involving and magical it becomes.

On CD 2, track 5, you can sample the scene in the dead-house, set for narrator and chorus, which describes the ghost pounding on the door (*Buch, Buch, Buch*), his attempts to raise the corpse to open it from inside, and the first two prayers (described by the narrator) of the girl to keep the body lying on its slab. The third prayer, cleverly, becomes the next number and is the big final aria for the soprano herself. Dvořák's quasi-cartoonish approach to this gory story is far more sophisticated in realizing the different levels at which the plot operates than it would be if he had tried to create a modern, expressionist nightmare.

The extract begins with ominous rumblings in the basses (remember them: they will reappear in *The Water Goblin* in exactly the same context); then the narrator and chorus sing a stylized folk ballad, complete with a catchy, if ominous, rhythmic refrain in the full orchestra (first heard at 2:01). This conveys both the menace of the situation and the macabre fun in hearing about it. First performed in England in 1885, Gilbert and Sullivan may have had this music in mind when they came up with their own Gothic horror operetta, *Ruddigore,* two years later (particularly such numbers as "Sir Rupert Murgatroyd" or "When the Night Wind Howls"). Sullivan, by the way, had plenty of personal experience of Dvořák, as he shared conducting responsibilities with the Czech composer during his 1885 London concerts, including the one at which the Seventh Symphony was premiered.

The Specter's Bride has never quite vanished from the repertoire, particularly in Czech cities, and like Dvořák's other choral works intended for the United Kingdom, it was published with texts in somewhat creaky English. Since it lasts only a bit longer than a typical performance of Beethoven's Ninth Symphony, there is no reason why it should not provide a welcome novelty in today's concert halls. There is just one proviso: it needs to be performed like the ghost story it is, which means with vigor and a certain ghoulish relish, an exceptionally keen focus on its orchestral color, and a touch of exaggeration at its climaxes. Then the music really comes into its own.

St. Ludmila

Saint who?

This is the least known of all of Dvořák's choral works and the most problematic in terms of modern performance. The idea for it may have come from Liszt's oratorio *The Legend of St. Elizabeth,* which Dvořák played under Smetana in 1866 (see "Dvořák Timeline"). Although written, like *The Specter's Bride,* for performance in England, the subject is Czech and nationalistic: the conversion of the Czech people to Christianity. The musical style, in which Dvořák's personal voice mingles a bit with that of Handel and Mendelssohn, is naturally eclectic. Like grand opera, the oratorio genre had its conventions that audiences of the day expected would be honored, and Dvořák prided himself on his ability to work within them. This was for him a pioneering effort in any case, the first great Czech sacred oratorio (and maybe the last as well, at least as far as the international choral repertoire is concerned).

It was important to Dvořák to demonstrate the universality of Czech music, just as he wanted to prove to his fellow countrymen that foreign elements could be used legitimately in creating a national style. *St. Ludmila* has thus become a victim of a particularly acute form of that paradox facing a number of Dvořák's operas: what was new locally (and just what the English audience ordered in this case) was bound to be seen as derivative and lacking in originality everywhere else. This judgment, combined with the fact that romantic sacred oratorios in general are considered even more hopelessly passé than French grand opera, has sealed *St. Ludmila*'s fate. And yet, everyone who hears it comes away with virtually the same impression: the music is excellent and impressively sustained. As the next work written after the epic Seventh Symphony, how could it not be?

The story is simple: Pagan Czechs are celebrating their annual spring festival by worshipping their local deities. The ax-wielding Holy Hermit Ivan shows up and smashes their idol, and Princess Ludmila, although horrified, is drawn to him by his message that there is only one God. With her skeptical servant Svatana, she seeks out Ivan in his wilderness retreat, where he explains to her the meaning of the Christian religion. Their meeting is interrupted by a party of hunters led by Prince Bořivoj (accompanied by a particularly evocative chorus). He has shot a doe, which

Ivan heals and restores to life. Impressed by this miracle, and even more by the presence of the (naturally) attractive Ludmila, Bořivoj resolves to learn of the one true God as well, and in the oratorio's final part, the two are baptized as Christians (and with them their people) and united in marriage.

It's simple, but not short. The entire work plays for about two and a half hours, and Dvořák realized early on that a complete performance was only possible on very special occasions, despite the fact that (as recordings prove) the music has all of his characteristic melodic appeal. Like the Stabat Mater, if on a larger scale, it is smartly arranged so that the first part is the longest and parts two and three grow progressively shorter. The various parts are also well differentiated, with two comparatively static tableaux (the pagan spring festival and the baptism ceremony) enclosing the more operatic, dramatic central story of the meeting between Ludmila and Bořivoj.

The orchestration is slightly larger than in *The Specter's Bride*. There's no piccolo, and Dvořák limits additional percussion to the triangle, but he adds a third trumpet, contrabassoon, and the organ, which is used with exceptional discretion as a contrasting instrumental color (as always in these works) and never in a way that makes the music sound bombastic or excessively "churchy." Indeed, the score truly is a marvel of economy and acute musical judgment. It's remarkable to hear how, for example, in the concluding chorus, Dvořák achieves a gloriously rich and full sound without ever straining for effect. Using the same orchestra found in such classical-period works as Schubert's Ninth Symphony (only double winds with no extras, no organ, and limiting the trumpets and horns to pairs) the impression he creates is both grand and spiritually luminous.

Over the course of its performance history, Dvořák made suggestions for cuts to encourage more frequent performances. *St. Ludmila,* like most grand operas or any number of oratorios by Handel, is not a work in which every note must be regarded as sacrosanct. Most interestingly, in 1901 Dvořák adapted the piece for stage performance, which meant adding some music (including the exciting moment in which Ivan summons lightening to destroy the statue of the pagan god, previously described indirectly), linking a few numbers and sanctioning a very large series of cuts and abridgments. This version has never been recorded, unfortunately, but it is readily available as part of the old Critical Edition of Dvořák's works. It would be very interesting to hear, because it might provide an ideal form of the piece, whether staged or not.

It remains to be seen if *St. Ludmila* can overcome what some perceive as the double handicap of a provincial subject (Czech) and a provincial treatment (English). During most of the twentieth century, the work was largely ignored even in Czechoslovakia because its Christian subject proved difficult for the country's communist authorities to stomach, despite (or even because of) its overall patriotic tone. Yet the oratorio was undoubtedly influential in its day. In England it was more highly praised than the later Requiem, and certainly the music's enlivening rhythmic thrust and tunefulness gave a shot in the arm to the sacred oratorio genre. It may be that with a newly democratic Czech Republic serving as a launching point, combined with a more tolerant and scholarly approach to the great choral works of the romantic period, *St. Ludmila* will at last have a chance to make its way in the world, at least occasionally. Certainly, on musical grounds alone, there's plenty to savor.

Mass in D

Originally composed for performance in a small, private chapel, this perfectly proportioned piece exists in two versions, one for chorus and organ, and the other scored for a smallish orchestra of two oboes, two bassoons, three horns, two trumpets, three trombones, timpani, organ, and strings. The brief solo parts can be sung by either individual singers or a few voices from the choir. In other words, the Mass is designed for both actual liturgical use and concert performance, and it works well either way. It lasts about forty minutes in total, and perhaps its closest analogue in terms of its understated style would be the celebrated Requiem of French composer Gabriel Fauré, where modesty of means never compromises sincerity of expression or shapeliness of form.

I would only mention one special feature of this piece as proof of the power of Dvořák's imagination, even in this comparatively tranquil and subdued context. The Credo has been the bane of all Mass writers since composers began combining voices and instruments. The text is the longest, and the succession of doctrinal clauses, with the exception of those that speak of the crucifixion and resurrection of Christ, suggests almost nothing in the way of musical treatment. Dvořák's solution to this problem strikes me as perhaps the most intelligent of anyone's. He sets the text as a responsorial dialogue between four alto or tenor voices and the larger choir. This masterstroke not only emphasizes the communal, ritualistic acceptance of Christian belief through the prayer service, but it also creates a natural musical process with a built-in sequence of contrasts and climaxes.

The Mass has not had an extensive history as a concert work, although it would make a welcome alternative to endless performances of the Fauré Requiem, and it may be that its best setting is the one for which it was originally intended: an actual church service. Nevertheless, it offers yet another example of Dvořák's uncanny ability to produce first-rate results, ideally tailored to local circumstances and practical needs. Its modesty, as Dvořák himself pointed out, needs no apology.

Requiem

This is the last and greatest of the choral works that Dvořák
composed for England and, amazingly, his next big project after
the sunny Eighth Symphony. It has never quite vanished from the
repertoire, but this, the romantic era's largest and grandest (if
not necessarily the loudest) setting of the Requiem Mass has been
the subject of much misunderstanding. The first misconception
concerns the work's overall length, which many commentators
exaggerate as though there's some upper limit beyond which
any setting of the Requiem is doomed to fail. In fact, the work
is only about fifteen minutes longer (on average) than Verdi's
Requiem and almost exactly the same duration as Mahler's Third
Symphony—about ninety-five to 100 minutes.

Now since the Mahler gets hauled out and performed
constantly, and its six movements conclude with a mostly hushed,
twenty-five-minute-long adagio requiring great patience and
concentration from its listeners, there's no reason that modern
audiences should not enjoy a thirteen-movement choral work as
highly varied in content as this. It's also worth mentioning that at
the premiere in Birmingham in 1891, the Requiem was only the
first item on a program that included Wagner's prelude to *Parsifal*
and Beethoven's Seventh Symphony. Concerts have become
progressively shorter since then, but only to the extent that a
major work like this one can now have a full evening to itself.

The second misconception stems from the contention that an
affable guy like Dvořák was not up to the emotional demands of
the text, particularly the depiction of the Day of Judgment (the
Dies Irae), which is not quite as theatrically hysterical as Verdi's.
Actually, Dvořák's setting, the most frightening of all of his train
tunes, is quite effective as it stands—especially given an organ
with strong pedal notes, a conductor willing to let the brass
strut their stuff, and the seldom-heard random clangor of bells

that Dvořák suggests accompany the "Tuba miram" section when heard the second time. The music is powered by the very same five-note motive that energizes the first movement of the First Symphony. So rather than judging the Requiem by inappropriate standards in the first place, it makes more sense to consider what Dvořák actually does, on its own merits, with the occasional sidelong glance at Verdi merely for purposes of orientation—not to say that one work is inherently superior to the other.

Dvořák's conception of the Requiem places the greatest weight on the chorus, while Verdi gives primary responsibility to the soloists. Dvořák's orchestration is also larger and more varied (although again not "better"—Verdi's is famously stunning). He requires two flutes plus piccolo; two clarinets plus bass clarinet; two oboes plus English horn; two bassoons plus contrabassoon; four trumpets, four horns, three trombones; and tuba, timpani, harp, tam-tam, (optional) bells, organ, and strings. Verdi's "Dies Irae" chorus is short and compact, not least because he repeats it three times. Dvořák's, on the other hand, is longer and more extensively developed, and he repeats it only twice, the second time more powerfully and with greater intensity than the first (Verdi's corresponding presentations are virtually identical).

The form of the Dvořák Requiem is more tightly knit than Verdi's, which makes sense given its composer's symphonic credentials. Think of it as resembling the shape of a large suspension bridge: two introductory movements lead to the section in which the twofold repetition of the "Dies Irae" chorus stands like the first pair of towers supporting the bridge's central, arching span. At the other end of the main arch, two repetitions of the "Quam olim Abraham" fugue constitute the second pair of choral "towers," while the last three movements gradually lead back to the mood of the opening. The opposition and placement of these choruses is critical to the expressive contrast at the heart of the piece: the terror of the Day of Judgment and the despair of death, as opposed to God's promise of redemption to the children of Abraham.

Unlike Verdi, who cleverly uses the "Dies Irae" chorus in the Requiem's last part to tie together his otherwise sprawling structure, Dvořák creates unity symphonically, by opening the work with a lyrical motto that reappears at critical points and generates much of the music's tension through various easily recognizable transformations (much as in the Eighth Symphony). You might well say that it represents death, for this is how the composer's son-in-law Josef Suk used it in his epic *Asrael Symphony* (Asrael is the Angel of Death), an often-despairing work composed in the wake of a double tragedy: the loss of both Dvořák and his daughter, Suk's wife.

As a representation of death, this motto does its job admirably. It is chromatic: that is, it defines no firm key, and so acts as a destabilizing element whenever it appears. It is this motto, rather than the terror represented by the "Dies Irae" chorus alone, that helps widen the work's expressive range. Dvořák opens and closes the piece with it, and so powerful is its influence that this is the only major Requiem setting in the entire romantic period that does *not* conclude with a message of consolation. Instead, the hope of eternal peace slowly, shockingly drains away, leaving in its wake a musical question mark and a final warning in the shape of an icy minor chord on the woodwinds.

At the exact center of the work, the seventh movement, stands the chorus "Confutatis maledictis," the words of which beg God not to abandon the souls of the faithful when the damned are cast into the fiery pit. Once again Dvořák's conception differs from most others, in that the subsequent prayer for salvation (after the vicious opening consigning the sinners to their just desserts) is accompanied not by music of solace and confidence in divine protection, but rather with intimations of fear and doubt in the form of the motto theme. At the last moment, the orchestra concludes on a positive note, only to have this immediately contradicted by the equally fretful "Lacrimosa," which speaks further of the judgment of the guilty, and ends in despair with the motto theme underpinned by ominous repetitions on solo timpani of the rhythmic motive of the "Dies Irae."

Far from being unable to rise to the expressive challenge of the text, Dvořák's setting in fact digs deeper into the darker emotional possibilities offered by the words than most others. That final appearance of the motto at the Requiem's conclusion has an effect similar to the unflinching victory of fate in the last movement of Mahler's Sixth Symphony, or the starkly grim and unsentimental conclusion to Sibelius's Fourth. Like those works, the Requiem represents a singular moment in its composer's output due to its emotional ambivalence and recurring sense of disquiet—its optimism constantly questioned, undermined, and ultimately negated.

To hear just how vividly Dvořák's symphonic conception supports the words, turn to CD 2, track 6, which presents the complete ninth movement ("Offertorium") of the Requiem. This section lasts about twelve minutes and begins with a solemn prelude for winds alone. The bass clarinet, in particular, colors the music with a dark, rich timbre. Then follows the first line of the prayer, set by Dvořák in the form of an invocation (at 1:38):

Domine Jesu Christe, Rex gloriae,   Lord Jesus Christ, King of glory,

This is sung as a flowing chant, first by the basses, then expanded by solo alto accompanied by muted strings and harp, and ending with a cry of "Rex gloriae" by the tenors and basses of the chorus. The entire passage is then repeated with the voices inverted (2:29): altos have the choral chant, the solo bass its expansion, and the choral sopranos and altos close the invocation. The upper voices of the chorus then repeat the entire five-word phrase in triumph one last time (3:20), ending with a last "Rex gloriae" from the tenors and basses.

The chorus next chants the first two words of the next clause, followed by solo soprano singing the rest (at 3:56):

libera animas omnium fidelium defunctorum de poenis inferni, et de profundo lacu:　　deliver the faithful souls of all who died from the pains of hell and from the deep abyss.

Notice the apt word setting (4:12) at the words "de poenis inferni." The chorus repeats the opening words of this phrase in a monotone, as the four soloists develop the entire thought in an impassioned ensemble. They make as if to move on directly to the next phrase in tandem with the chorus (04:58), repeating the words "libera eas" with increasing urgency:

libera eas de ore leonis, ne absorbeat eas tartarus, ne cadant in obscurum:　　deliver them from the lion's maw, let hell not swallow them, nor let them fall into darkness.

Before the singers can continue, however, the motto theme intervenes plaintively on oboe followed by English horn (5:29) and plunges the ensemble into a passage of deep anxiety aptly capturing the sense of the above text:

sed signifer sanctus Michael repraesentet eas in lucem sanctam:　　let Saint Michael lead them forth into Thy holy light:

This next clause begins more confidently (6:43), leading to the same music that accompanied the final appearance of the opening invocation (7:24). Then follows the glorious choral fugue that concludes the movement (8:02):

Quam olim Abraham promisisti, et semini ejus.　　As Thou promised of old to Abraham and to his seed.

The tune of this fugue is as catchy as a folk song, and its treatment ecstatically joyous as it rises from one thrilling climax to the next.

There's not a note here that falls below Dvořák's highest standards. The Requiem is also one of those works (like Mahler's Third Symphony, in fact) that increases in stature the more familiar you become with it. This is because in order to experience its maximum emotional impact, it has to be heard in terms of its immediate, moment-by-moment content as well as perceived whole, as a large-scale structure following a very skillfully planned expressive trajectory. In other words, the music is unusually subtle, technically sophisticated, and surprisingly disturbing, all things that so many assume that Dvořák is not.

Unfortunately, it's almost axiomatic that when a composer writes a work that runs counter to the prevailing simplistic assumptions about him, it's easier and more common to criticize the work than it is to question the truth of those assumptions. Beyond that, most people understand that traditionally a Requiem setting, even one for concert use only, will at least convey a message of hope and consolation. The fact that Dvořák's does not may also have something to do with its relative infrequency of performance. Still, since music rich in expressive ambivalence is often considered praiseworthy in other composers, surely Dvořák also deserves credit for what he achieves in this epic, moody, and emotionally gripping piece.

Te Deum

There are four great musical settings from the classical period to the present of this joyful song of praise: Haydn's, Verdi's, Bruckner's, and this one. Despite the fact that Dvořák told Jeannette Thurber of the National Conservatory in New York that he thought the poem of *The American Flag* "grand," he claimed that he did not have time to set it to music before his arrival in New York. So he wrote a masterpiece instead. Just about everyone who knows this work agrees in that estimation of it, but it's still very seldom performed—a terrible pity, because in twenty short minutes, it offers more fun that you probably ever believed possible in a sacred choral work.

The opening is more than happy: it's gleeful to the point of being humorous, thanks to being both polyrhythmic and syncopated. Timpani begin solo, pounding out a triplet rhythm. Over this, strings play the principal theme of the entire work in duple rhythm, and on top of that, the chorus chimes in with the first words of the text, "We praise thee, O God." This mounts in vigor, percussion crashing and bashing with uninhibited abandon. The full orchestration consists of pairs of flutes, oboes, clarinets, bassoons, and trumpets; with four horns, three trombones and tuba, English horn, bass drum, cymbals, triangle, and strings. Wonderful as this opening is in making "a joyful noise unto the Lord," it also happens to be the rhythmic twin of the scherzo in the F Minor Piano Trio, No. 3.

Dvořák asks for only two soloists, a soprano and a bass, and he quite unusually divides the work into four sections similar to those of a short symphony (although the form of each movement is dictated by the sense of the text). Here's how Dvořák lays out the piece:

First Movement
Opening chorus (fast); soprano solo with chorus (slow); reprise of opening chorus (fast)

Second Movement
Brass fanfare introducing a bass solo with chorus (slow)

Third Movement
Chorus (fast)

Fourth Movement
Soprano solo with chorus (modified reprise of first-movement
solo); soprano and bass duet with choral shouts of "Alleluia,"
leading to a reprise of the opening and a quick, brash, jolly coda

The Te Deum has gained a measure of popularity in recent
years, particularly on recordings, perhaps because its barbaric
splendor and energy so clearly anticipate the similar exuberance
of the enthralling Glagolitic Mass by Dvořák's younger colleague
and friend, Leoš Janáček. It concludes what is not only the finest
collection of large-scale concert works on Latin sacred texts
composed in the entire nineteenth century, but also the last
such corpus by any of the generally acknowledged great classical
composers. The fact that this type of music seems to be out of
fashion at present should not be allowed to diminish Dvořák's
accomplishment. A deeply spiritual man and a sincere believer
all his life, he is also one of the very few musicians of the period
who knew the difference between religion and religiosity, and
how to endow his sacred music with the former while remaining
refreshingly free of the latter.

Miscellaneous Orchestral Works

Dvořák's output of orchestral works is unparalleled in terms of quality, variety, and quantity. A brief glance at the list on the following page reveals a sufficient number of popular favorites and repertory standards for this point to need no additional reinforcement. If you take a glance at the scoring of each work, however, you will discover two useful facts about his use of the symphony orchestra. First, although the orchestration of many of them is, on the whole, larger than that of the symphonies, Dvořák seldom asks for more than a standard, well-equipped ensemble of his day might be able to provide. There are never more than two trumpets (with one exception) and never more than the standard four horns, or double winds. He was above all being practical: he wanted his music to be widely played, and so it needed to pose no special logistical problems.

On the other hand, his love of instrumental color is just as readily apparent. Compared to the symphonies, note the frequency of instruments such as the harp, as well as the extra woodwind instruments (piccolo, English horn, and bass clarinet). Still interesting is Dvořák's general avoidance of the contrabassoon (indeed of the three works listed that ask for it, two mark the part as optional, although it should always be used). Only a single piece, however, save for the special case of the serenades, has timpani alone *without* additional percussion, while most at

Dvořák: Miscellaneous Orchestral Works

	Flute + Piccolo	Oboe + English Horn	Clarinet + Bass Clarinet	Bassoons + Contra- bassoon
Serenades/Suites				
Serenade for Strings				
Serenade for Winds		2	2	2+1
Slavonic Dances	2+1	2	2	2
Czech Suite	2	2+1	2	2
Legends	2	2	2	2
"American" Suite	2+1	2	2	2+1
Single-Movement Works				
Symphonic Variations	2+1	2	2	2
Slavonic Rhapsody No. 1	2+1	2	2	2
Slavonic Rhapsody No. 2	2	2	2	2
Slavonic Rhapsody No. 3	2+2	2	2	2
Scherzo Capriccioso	2+1	2+1	2+1	2
Concert Overtures				
Dramatic Overture	2+1	2+1	2	2
My Home	2	2	2	2
Hussite	2+1	2+1	2	2
Symphonic Poems				
Symphonic Poem, Op. 18	2+1	2+1	2	2
In Nature's Realm	2	2+1	2+1	2
Carnival	2+1	2+1	2	2
Othello	2+1	2+1	2	2
The Noonday Witch	2+1	2	2+1	2
The Water Goblin	2+1	2+1	2+1	2
The Golden Spinning Wheel	2+1	2+1	2	2+1
The Wood Dove	2+1	2+1	2+1	2
The Hero's Song	2	2	2	2

Horns	Trumpets	Trombones + Tuba	Percussion* + Misc.	Harp
(strings only)				
3			cello + bass	
4	2	3	C + glockenspiel	
2	2		A	
4	2		B	1
4	2	3+1	C	
4	2	3	B	
4	2	3	C	
4	2	3	C	1
4	2	3	C	2 (1)
4	2	3+1	C	1
4	2	3+1	C	1
4	2	3	B	
4	2	3+1	C	1
4	2	3+1	C	1
4	2	3+1	B + cymbals	
4	2	3+1	B + cymbals; tambourine	1
4	2	3+1	C w/o triangle	1
4	2	3+1	C + bell	
4	2	3+1	C + tam-tam; bell	
4	2	3+1	C	1
4	2	3+1	C + tambourine; 3 offstage trumpets	1
4	2	3+1	C	

* A = timpani　　B = timpani and triangle　　C = timpani and triangle, bass drum, cymbals

least use bass drum, cymbals, and triangle. A similar lavishness is found in only one symphony (the Fourth).

Later in his career, Dvořák developed an increasing fondness for quiet percussive effects, the swoosh of suspended cymbals above all. So the watchword in all these pieces is maximum variety and timbral flexibility, with the most economical and practical scoring possible. However, before moving on to a brief consideration of these works in turn, you may well ask yourself an interesting question: Why is it that the orchestration of the symphonies is comparatively more restrained? The reason for this isn't difficult to understand, and it provides an enlightening perspective on the evolution of symphonic music in general that's well worthy taking a moment to discuss.

Dvořák, as you saw, had great experience in playing in opera orchestras. These ensembles commonly used extra instruments such as English horns, harps, and percussion in illustrating the action happening on stage. The English horn, for example, might be associated with reed pipes or the rustic character of a shepherd. Harps conjure up celestial imagery and the sweet tones of love music. Percussion, in the form of cymbals and drums, naturally accompanies battles, storms, and scenes of violence. The dark tam-tam (or gong) represents death, hell, or evil forces, while tambourines and castanets convey local color in the form of folk music and dancing.

To the ears of nineteenth-century listeners, the use of these instruments might well signify concrete images: that is, actual "things" rather than abstract emotions. Symphonies and concertos, on the other hand, are supposed to be about the pure expression of feelings. Anything that detracts from this, that asks the listener to say, "That sounds like a bird, or a battle, or a love scene," detracts from the method by which composers were supposed to achieve this depth of expression: the dramatic interaction and development of themes and not by special instrumental effects.

The first romantic composer who found a way to integrate a purportedly extramusical vocabulary of sounds and images into a symphonic musical discourse was Mahler, and his achievement in this respect was extremely controversial and even now remains little recognized. Dvořák not only belonged to an earlier generation, he had a practical financial need to achieve rapid success as a composer (he was not a soloist or conductor and had a large family to feed). He could not afford to be a radical like Wagner, notoriously famous as a pamphleteer, but seldom performed, and supported by the erratic charity of a loony monarch. Dvořák's strongly classical leanings in any case led him to maintain the distinction between programmatic and absolute music. He pushed the envelope as far as he felt it would go in his symphonies, as I have already suggested, but he respected the basic separation of genres. Rather than write symphonies full of novel orchestral effects, he simply stopped writing them altogether and switched to symphonic poems.

Dvořák did this (from an aesthetic point of view) partly because, like most composers working in the 1890s, he could no longer square the advances in the coloristic possibilities of the modern orchestra, freely used and accepted in opera, with conservative views regarding symphonies and concertos that appeared increasingly outmoded, inhibiting, and aesthetically irrelevant (not to mention German). He was also concerned that Czech music, which effectively meant his own, should remain current with the latest trends. What, after all, would be the point of achieving a national school of music, of catching up to the most advanced European cultures in every genre and form, only to fall behind through blind adherence to a stale aesthetic system?

Had Dvořák been born twenty years later, he might have done as his Czech compatriot Mahler did: toss everything into the pot and call the result a symphony. Instead, he gave up the form in which he earned the most international acclaim, and so showed both his colleagues and the world that Czech music could be as technically and aesthetically modern as any. I don't want to exaggerate the saintliness of this act or portray it as some form of epic sacrifice. The decision obviously suited Dvořák's own perception of the direction in which his personal artistic growth was heading, and the evidence of his actions certainly suggests that he was extremely self-aware in this respect.

However, even granting the basic fact that he knew exactly what he was doing in terms of his own inner development, Dvořák's focus at the end of his life on symphonic poems and operas was much more than a desperate bid for popularity in a field in which he had enjoyed only limited success to date. It was a lesson to his countrymen that the way forward could never be the path of narrow-minded provincialism or ideological rigidity. Given the exceptional success and mastery of his last symphonies and chamber works, and the ease with which he could have continued to capitalize on it, the path he chose was more than a little selfless. But as the extensive list of his orchestral works shows, it was also a move that he had been preparing himself to make all his life.

Serenades and Suites

Serenade for Strings (1875)
Serenade for Winds (1878)
Slavonic Dances (1878 and 1887)
Czech Suite (1879)
Legends (1881)
"American" Suite (1895)

Dvořák's two serenades have been popular since their first performances, as well as universally acclaimed as light music of the finest quality. Despite the differences in orchestration, both share a use of cyclical form, with the opening theme of the first movement (and in the String Serenade, the slow movement as well) returning just before the end of the finale.

The Wind Serenade is perhaps the more widely admired of the two, often mentioned as the only composition in the entire repertoire that can stand comparison to Mozart's great works in the genre, and it represents a most loving tribute to the centuries-long tradition of Bohemian woodwind playing, a school that still exists today. The melodies of all four movements come from Dvořák's top drawer, beginning with a lively march followed by a slow dance (enclosing a quick one with typically Czech syncopated rhythms). The heart of the work is the slow movement, in which Dvořák achieves amazingly long, sensuous, singing lines and an aching melancholy of Mozartian finesse, while the finale does an excellent impersonation of a village band. Seldom has genius expressed itself more amiably and with less pretentiousness.

The String Serenade is the first in a triumvirate of great nineteenth-century contributions to what became a very popular genre (especially in England from the turn of the twentieth century onwards), the other two being Tchaikovsky's Serenade for Strings (1881), and the string orchestra arrangement of Grieg's *Holberg Suite* (1885). Dvořák's piece has five movements: a wistful introduction with a middle section that comes very close in its primal simplicity to the music of his American period, an elegant waltz anticipating the similar movement in the Eighth Symphony, a lively scherzo, a heartfelt slow movement with particularly luscious themes, and a lively finale in folk style with a very humorous second subject. Composed before Dvořák's official Slavonic period, like the scherzo of the Second Symphony, this piece reminds the listener that the various styles and musical voices that he adopted at different times and for various works were in fact present all along.

There's little that needs to be said about the Slavonic Dances, which are generally acknowledged as the finest works of their type. Two points are worth stressing: first, unlike their models (Brahms's Hungarian Dances), all of Dvořák's tunes are completely original, even though they may sound so much like folk music as to be easily mistaken for the real thing. Second, Dvořák refused the title Czech Dances, suggested by his publisher Simrock—interestingly preferring instead to cast a wider net and include representative dance forms from all over Eastern Europe. The result of this catholicity not only highlights his desire not to be limited by national labels, it reflects his deliberate intention from the very outset of his professional career to achieve success on an international scale.

The first, earlier set of dances is characterized by its almost primal vigor. Dance No. 7 became a very memorable segment in the animated film *Allegro non troppo* (a sort of *Fantasia* for grownups), while No. 2 had a noticeable influence on the second of Elgar's *Pomp and Circumstance* marches. The second set, which Dvořák had to be pushed into writing at all, reveals greater sophistication in the orchestration (particularly in the more subtle use of percussion) with no loss of melodic appeal. You can hear just how instantly memorable this music is on CD 2, track 7, which contains the Fifth Dance from the second set (Op. 72). I include this dance not only because its tunes are thrilling (check out the varied reprise of the opening at 1:18) but because only a few of the dances get played nowadays, mostly as encores, which means that little gems such as this one remain relatively (and scandalously) unknown outside of recordings.

Although this is light music, at least technically, a performance of either set (or all sixteen) would make an excellent concert work in its own right. There isn't a single dull note or dead spot in any of these pieces, which also exist (and initially became famous) in their "home" versions for piano duet. They further inspired an endless host of later works, from composers such as Bartók and Kodály in Hungary and Malcolm Arnold in England, while remaining the standard by which all other such efforts are still measured. The Slavonic Dances, above all, represent a breathtaking achievement in the fine art of melody, and they have that special quality of perennial, unfading freshness that very few other works can match.

The *Czech Suite* is something of a musical landmark, although it is seldom recognized as such. Its five movements, each distinctively scored, are:

Praeludium (pastorale)	2 oboes, 2 bassoons, 2 horns, strings
Polka	2 oboes, 2 bassoons, 2 horns, strings
Menuett (sousedská)	2 flutes, 2 clarinets, 2 bassoons, strings
Romanze	2 flutes, 2 oboes, English horn, 2 bassoons, 2 horns, strings
Finale (furiant)	full ensemble (including trumpets and timpani)

Note the severely baroque/classical restraint of the orchestration, especially the Mozartian clarinets in the third movement. On the other hand, the soulful English horn solo in the romanze looks forward not just to the "New World" Symphony but also to the writing for the same instrument in the romanza of English composer Ralph Vaughan Williams's Fifth Symphony (1943). This movement of Dvořák's, with its haunting modal harmony and a tune so beautiful you could cry, also sounds as if it could be a piece of early incidental music by Sibelius (a lost movement of the *Karelia Suite,* perhaps?)

However, the really important point is that this is the very first example (I believe) of a baroque/classical suite format in which the traditional prelude and dance movements are replaced by their ethnic/national equivalents. It's exactly the sort of thing found much later in the twentieth-century neoclassical works of such composers as Heitor Villa-Lobos (*Bachianas Brasileiras*), Julián Orbón (*Tres versiones sinfónicas*), Gustav Holst (*St. Paul's Suite*), and too many others to name here.

It's also surely significant that this is the only orchestral work that Dvořák ever wrote that contains the word *Czech* in its title. What he is doing, particularly in the movements with double headings, is demonstrating that Czech music belongs naturally to the great international tradition of the baroque and classical masters. He did exactly the same thing in the deliberately traditionally structured scherzo of the Sixth Symphony. Although to some extent characteristic of Dvořák's entire life's work, it would be difficult to imagine this idea demonstrated with more artless charm than in this sunny, winning piece. It deserves to be better known.

Dvořák's last major work for the ensemble known today as a chamber orchestra is *Legends,* which also exists in the form of a piano duet. The entire selection of ten movements plays for about forty minutes, and like the *Czech Suite,* it seems to have practically vanished from concert programs, unaccountably because (yet again) just about everyone who knows this music agrees about its exceptional quality. Even the title is singularly apt: Dvořák doesn't give any indication as to what, if anything, these little nuggets of musical poetry describe, but he encourages each listener to bring his or her own imagination to bear. Although the orchestra is small, you can see from the table that almost no two works requires the same forces.

Note the sensitivity of Dvořák's ear here. He contrasts the most heavily scored piece (*No. 4*) with the lightest (*No. 5*). The sound of the harp adds a touch of contrasting color at the work's dead center (*Nos. 5* and *6*). The orchestration of the second half is less varied than the first, with the last pair of numbers echoing the sonorities of the previous two. This creates an entirely

Dvořák: *Legends* (Scoring Including Strings)

No.	Flute	Oboe	Clarinet	Bassoons	Horns	Trumpets	Timpani	Triangle	Harp
1	2	2	2	2	4		yes		
2	1	2	2	2	4				
3	2	2	2	2	4			yes	
4	2	2	2	2	4	2	yes	yes	
5	2	2	2	2	2				yes
6	2	2	2	2	2				yes
7	2	2	2	2	2		yes		
8	2	2	2	2	4				
9	2	2	2	2	2		yes		
10	2	2	2	2	4				

natural and subtle sense of finality when you hear the entire set at a sitting. Musical analysis often founders when it tries to take into account the significance of sheer sound, or instrumental timbre, as an organizational principal (unless this is really obvious, like a movement for just strings followed by one for just woodwinds). But Dvořák, like Mahler and a few other composers, really did use timbre in a way that often has structural implications.

Try to get a sense of the music's poetic qualities as you listen to *Legend No. 6,* on CD 2, track 8. First, note how the accompaniment, a constant stream of triplets in the harp, actually generates the melody, which begins in the violins and cellos with the same rhythm and then grows in lyrical expansiveness. The two clarinets echo each initial phrase of the melody, and this four-note echo itself becomes the second important idea (at 0:25), which also expands naturally from the seeds of its first few phrases. This leads back to the first theme on the violas and cellos (1:17), the harp resuming its triplet rhythm.

As the melody fades away, the violas keep up the steady pulse of the harp, and the clarinets start another tune (1:38) derived from the "dum, dum, dadum" rhythm that ends the opening theme's first phrase. Unlike the previous two themes, this one remains stuck in short phrases, until suddenly (2:08) the violins interrupt with an enchanting new idea: it's the half-rustic, half-heroic tune from the middle section of the Third Symphony's slow movement. What's remarkable here, lending credence to the idea that Dvořák actually thought in instrumental terms, is that he preserves the same orchestration of this theme as in the symphony. Strings sing out the first phrase, while the solo clarinet has the continuation (2:20), and in both cases, the accompaniment features the harp.

This tune gradually leads back to the opening (3:05), only now the strings have the triplet rhythm in the form of a countermelody, while flutes, clarinets, and bassoons have the main theme. Dvořák skips the middle section, instead cutting straight to the reprise on violas and cellos with the accompaniment back in the harp (3:26). Violins take over from the original clarinets and whisper the third tune (3:35), and this gradually expands under the steady triplet rhythm of the strings into a gentle coda, giving the last word to the harp against soft chords on lower strings and woodwinds (except oboes). I can describe who plays what, but I can't even begin to convey what I can only call the music's "once upon a time" quality, that indefinable spirit that truly justifies the title of "Legend." I hope that you hear it too.

Dvořák's last suite for orchestra, the so-called "American" Suite (he simply called it Suite in A) began its life for piano but is best known in its orchestral garb. Like the Serenade for Strings, it has five movements, with a cyclical return of its opening theme just before the end. The bold, simple tunes clearly come from the composer's American period, while the orchestration, with contrabassoon and touches of suspended cymbal in the second movement, looks forward to the symphonic poems and operas to come. Pay particular attention to the theme of the finale, one of those three-repeated-note specials that Dvořák loved (witness the finale of the Fourth Symphony), and which make some people crazy on account of their rhythmic obstinacy. It's also the very last of his train tunes and, at the same time, a charming set of lazy, "do nothing" variations such as characterized the second half of the finale of the Eighth Symphony.

In sum, there's a lot of Dvořák in this witty little finale, and all I can say in such cases is that he invariably knew the difference between being childlike and being childish. The primitive feel of the music in this case is as intentional as it is in Stravinsky's *The Rite of Spring*. The suite can be characterized aptly as the essence of folk song as Dvořák understood it, all boiled down to a sort of universal common denominator. It makes a fitting conclusion to a collection of works of uniformly high quality, even though their individual representation on international concert stages is very far from equal.

Single-Movement Works

Symphonic Variations (1877)
Slavonic Rhapsody No. 1 (1878)
Slavonic Rhapsody No. 2 (1878)
Slavonic Rhapsody No. 3 (1878)
Scherzo Capriccioso (1883)

This group of pieces contains two of Dvořák's most highly acclaimed short orchestral works, as well as three barely known yet well-thought-of (considering their comparative anonymity) examples of his Slavonic style. Just why the three Slavonic Rhapsodies remain so neglected is a mystery. Although inspired by the Hungarian Rhapsodies of Liszt, Dvořák audibly surpassed his models. As the table of orchestrations on page 142 shows, each of the rhapsodies requires a slightly different distribution of forces, but these differences matter. The first is the most rustic and folklike, with a reedy emphasis on the woodwinds and an important rhythmic contribution from the timpani. Dvořák's writing for kettledrums, by the way, is usually conservative in terms of the number of notes he requires the player to use but is always extremely active rhythmically. He particularly loves timpani solos in quiet contexts where, as here, the instrument sounds extremely romantic and sonorous, especially in the poetic die-away ending.

The Second Rhapsody, the only one in a minor key (G minor), comes the closest in its gaunt, chromatic main theme to sounding like the Liszt of the Hungarian Rhapsodies, but the answer on the woodwinds, with its arresting harmonic shift, could only have come from the Czech composer. Dvořák omits the piccolo, an indication that the overall mood will likely be a shade darker, and so it proves. Of the three pieces, this is the most turbulent, with energetic passages for the full orchestra separated by lyrical interludes backed by the harp on the way to a very powerful conclusion.

Neither of these first two pieces is excessively long (about twelve minutes each), but the last of them adds a minute or two in most performances and makes a fittingly grand conclusion to the series. It has always been the most popular of the three rhapsodies and the most frequently recorded. Dvořák opens with a unison solo for two harps (one will do in a pinch). This apparently irritated Smetana, whose cycle of tone poems *My Country* (*Má Vlast*) also begins with a harp solo. Then again, the second act of Verdi's *Aida* starts similarly, and since that opera reached Prague in 1875, it's safe to assume that Dvořák knew it well enough to reassure himself that harp solos were not necessarily a Smetana exclusive.

The tone of this work is one of uninhibited high spirits, with both flutes taking piccolos at the finish to add an extra touch of brilliance to the already-sumptuous orchestral palette. Dvořák also includes, shortly before the end, another of those remarkable passages for strings playing eerie, metallic tremolos on the bridge of the instrument (*sul ponticello*). The rhapsody's second theme cuts the same dashing figure as the "big tune" in Berlioz's *Le Corsair* overture. Indeed, the work has a certain breezy French insouciance and verve that once again displays Dvořák's extensive knowledge of Offenbach, and operetta in general. Perhaps the only thing to be said against these delightful pieces is that they are, after all, rhapsodies, and so lack the formal cohesion of Dvořák's instrumental movements in more disciplined forms, but it's more than a little cheap to denigrate them for being exactly what they say they are.

Speaking of more disciplined forms, in the Symphonic Variations, we have not only one of Dvořák's most highly regarded masterpieces but also another work that had a huge impact on future composers. First the work itself: it consists of a single movement a bit over twenty minutes long containing twenty-seven variations on a short, curiously exotic-sounding original theme taken from a chorus called "I Am A Fiddler." This theme has a highly unusual and unforgettable shape: an opening phrase that always sounds a bar shorter than it ought to be (it takes seven measures, with solo timpani filling up the seventh), a middle section consisting of a rising wave of melody six measures long, and an identical repeat of the opening seven measures. Most melodies (from all musical eras) tend to fall into two-, four-, and eight-bar periods. This inner symmetry is practically hard-wired into our expectations as listeners, so the lopsided impression this oddly structured tune produces is very striking indeed.

Part of the genius in selecting this theme, then, lies in the fact that its truncated nature automatically undermines its sense of closure, and so inevitably leads the ear onward from one variation to the next. It also serves as an excellent pretext for several humorous moments. Nevertheless, because the melody is so brief, Dvořák groups the variations into larger paragraphs that provide additional continuity, and then concludes the whole with an exuberantly witty fugue based on the first part of the theme. To call the variations "imaginative" would be an understatement: the piece is a tour-de-force of its kind, although it was not recognized as such until it was first played in England in the early 1880s. Since then, it has remained reasonably well represented in concert as a repertory item, and it has also been frequently recorded.

As for its later influence, the list of subsequent "symphonic variations" or "variations for orchestra on an original theme" is very large, especially by English composers, and includes

Hubert Parry's Symphonic Variations, Samuel Coleridge Taylor's *Symphonic Variations on an African Air,* and most prominently, Edward Elgar's magnificent *Enigma Variations,* which features a theme of much greater length than Dvořák's, but one remarkably similar in shape. Elgar really knew his Dvořák, having played violin in the Sixth Symphony and the Stabat Mater under the composer's direction.

Turn now to the last work in this group, and jump ahead for a moment, to the winter of 1909. During his first season at the helm of what eventually became the New York Philharmonic, Gustav Mahler directed a concert in which he played Dvořák's horn-led Scherzo Capriccioso followed by Richard Strauss's even more famously horn-led tone poem *Till Eulenspiegel's Merry Pranks.* The pairing was not accidental. Mahler, who had a curiously competitive love-hate relationship with Strauss, doubtless enjoyed the tacit suggestion that a Czech nationalist of the older generation might have influenced Germany's greatest living composer and musical modernist.

Of course, Mahler could also simply have enjoyed the chance to place two curiously similar, humorous pieces in succession. It's a very intelligent bit of programming in any event, but it's also fun to speculate, not least because this same work of Dvořák's also shares a strong conceptual affinity with the hugely horn-led scherzo of Mahler's own Fifth Symphony. Consider in both cases, for instance, the use of the waltz: the contrast between the ebullient outer sections and the notably nocturnal, contemplative central episode, or the nostalgic reverie just before the wild coda. It's all very suggestive.

The idea of an independent symphonic scherzo (which means "joke"), alternately witty and romantically lyrical in tone, apparently originated with Dvořák in this unique work. In order to write a stand-alone scherzo some fourteen minutes in length, Dvořák had to go beyond the simple ABA form of most such movements, and while respecting it in the main, he enriches his design with a good bit of quite rigorous symphonic development. This is where both Mahler and Strauss come in, as well as Dvořák's own son-in-law Josef Suk (Fantastic Scherzo), Paul Dukas (*The Sorcerer's Apprentice*), Béla Bartók (Scherzo for Piano and Orchestra), Ernest Bloch (Scherzo Fantasque, for piano and orchestra), and others. It's not necessary to suggest the possibility of direct influence simply to note that Dvořák certainly was on to something here. Just what, you can hear for yourself on CD 2, track 9.

Much of the humor in this piece lies in the fact that for most of its length, it can't make up its mind what key it properly belongs in. Now since you can't really hear "key structure" as such, especially when the music is deliberately indecisive about it, Dvořák frames this dilemma as a series of instrumental questions about just how the opening theme ought to go. One of the lead comedians is the bass clarinet, whose rotund commentary punctuates the piece now and then like an embarrassing but funny gastric disturbance. As noted, the music begins with the solo horn tossing out the main theme, which is immediately questioned by everyone else, beginning with the cellos. Here is what happens afterwards:

0:29: The strings think they're on to something, and the whole orchestra bursts in with the theme accompanied by bass drum and cymbals, then harp and triangle, in alternating phrases (but in a key very different from that of the opening, if you have a particularly strong feel for these things).

0:55: Some more quizzical chirping from the winds and buzzing from the strings leads to a luscious, carefree waltz (also in quite a different key).

2:06: The waltz ultimately leads back to the beginning, only this time the uncertainty about the main theme is much stronger.

Eventually it arrives, late but enthusiastic as ever, and so proceeds once again to the waltz (note the goofy piccolo decorations—this time around at 3:37), and on to the middle (trio) section.

4:40: This begins with a haunting nocturne on the English horn, soon joined by the rest of the woodwinds.

5:45: The second half of the trio is another waltz on the strings, but one far more wistful, shortly reaching a passionate minor-key climax. The entire trio is then repeated.

8:16: Now comes a brief development section, in which the main themes appear in various combinations (note the horns and trumpets with bits of the principal tune against the wistful waltz in the strings).

8:50: Flute and bass clarinet initiate the recapitulation by entertaining each other with the main theme in a witty dialogue, and after still more development, this tune finally bursts out once again (at 10:01) in the full orchestra, accompanied as at the beginning by bass drum and cymbals, and then harp and triangle, but in a different harmonic position so that the tune sounds—well—the only word is "overenthusiastic."

10:36: The carefree waltz returns one last time, leading to a remarkable passage that sounds like a drugged memory of the work's various themes.

12:27: This dreamy but slightly warped contentment gives way to a solo harp cadenza that rouses the orchestra one last time, and the manic percussion section pounds the piece to a close with positively sadistic glee.

For much of the nineteenth and twentieth centuries, musical progress was (and still is) often measured largely in terms of the degree of aural pain regularly added to the modern musical vocabulary, as if happiness and joy were inherently superficial and unworthy of serious consideration. It's fitting, then, that

one of Dvořák's most prophetic gifts to later musical develop-
ments should be the emancipation of humor and the idea that
the expression of high spirits in terms of the romantic style can
be just as sophisticated and technically accomplished as it was in
Haydn's hands during the classical period.

Concert Overtures

Dramatic Overture (1870)
My Home (1881)
Hussite (1883)

The difference between a nineteenth-century *concert overture*
(that is, a stand-alone overture and not a prelude to a larger
theatrical work) and *symphonic poem* is often one of semantics.
Broadly speaking, concert overtures, unlike symphonic poems,
may be inspired by a theme or idea but do not tell a story or
attempt to convey concrete illustrative ideas. That's the theory
anyway. It falls apart completely when considering works such
as Beethoven's *Leonore Overture* No. 3, which is without question
a symphonic poem, and Strauss's *Also Sprach Zarathustra,* which
claims to be a tone poem (Strauss's preferred term) but isn't about
anything at all except in the vaguest symbolic sort of way.

Dvořák, like Mahler, sat on the fence in this regard, struggling
to figure out the limits of "absolute" music. It was an important
issue back in those days, because it inherently allied a composer
with either the Wagner or Brahms camp, and this could have
serious, career-making or -breaking results. This may be the
reason that Dvořák originally called his Symphonic Poem Op.
18 a rhapsody. Either way, it isn't about anything that he ever
let on. Similarly, when designating the unified trilogy of works
Nature, Life, and Love also as *In Nature's Realm, Carnival,* and *Othello,*

he called them overtures but insisted to his publisher that they were genuine program music, which is why I place them with the symphonic poems that follow. That leaves three indisputable concert overtures.

As I mentioned in discussing the operas, the *Dramatic Overture* (or *Tragic Overture,* as it's sometimes called) is actually the revised prelude to Dvořák's first opera, *Alfred.* It was never performed in his lifetime, and it reveals the composer's fascination with the Bacchanal from Wagner's *Tannhäuser* overture. The mixture of chromatic harmony with Dvořák's own, less cloudy idiom makes for some surprising contrasts, and it would be idle to pretend that this piece finds him at his most memorable. That said, it's certainly enjoyable, and it does live up to its title, being moody and turbulent, with plenty of German-sounding heroic striving. Perhaps the worst thing you can say about it is that the bits of recognizable Dvořák tend to rub shoulders uneasily with the rest; in other words, its various elements have not been all that well integrated.

The other two concert overtures, *My Home* and *Hussite,* are both overtly patriotic works, and they belong among the very few pieces by Dvořák that borrow pre-existing themes, although in neither case are these folk tunes. In *My Home,* which began life as part of a larger incidental score, the melody is that of a patriotic song. In the *Hussite Overture,* it's the famous chorale "Ye Who Are Warriors of God," happily beginning with three repeated notes so that it sounds just like Dvořák anyway. It is also used (overused, to be frank) in the last two symphonic poems of Smetana's epic cycle *Má Vlast.*

Both works, like all Dvořák in patriotic mode, are more noteworthy for their spontaneity and rhythmic vigor than for their bombast and posturing, although the spectacular ending to *Hussite* obviously intends to bring the house down, and does just that. Dvořák enjoyed conducting this work abroad, making it a sort of musical calling card establishing his credentials as a Czech patriot. He included the work on the program of his first London concert in 1884, and if you enjoy Elgar, it's easy to hear that the moods and textures of this piece made an indelible impression on him. *My Home* also has a noteworthy athleticism and drive, surprisingly lithe and airy for an avowedly nationalistic piece, and very similar in fact to some of Beethoven's more festive overtures, such as *The Consecration of the House.*

Symphonic Poems

Symphonic Poem (Rhapsody) in A Minor, Op. 18 (1874)
In Nature's Realm (1891)
Carnival (1891)
Othello (1892)
The Noonday Witch (1896)
The Water Goblin (1896)
The Golden Spinning Wheel (1896)
The Wood Dove (1896)
The Hero's Song (1897)

Few people realize that Dvořák wrote exactly as many symphonic poems as he did symphonies—nine of each—although the confusion in nomenclature partly accounts for this fact. I mentioned in the previous section that symphonic poems generally fall into two types: those inspired by specific scenes, events, or objects, and those that attempt to actually tell a story though some form of orchestral narrative process. Dvořák's output encompasses both, and apparently one other as well: the symphonic poem about nothing at all. Doubtless this lack of specificity has prevented Op. 18 from achieving the exposure it deserves, because it's a fine piece: a big, sprawling, passionate hunk of urgent romantic expression very much in the style of the opera *Vanda,* which dates from the following year.

The scoring is quite voluptuous and modern-sounding (for the period), with prominent harp passages and Dvořák's most systematic use of soft, hairpin crescendo rolls on the bass drum, an effect possibly gleaned from the "Storm" scene in the final act of Verdi's *Rigoletto.* The whole piece, in fact, has an urgency and sweep, a theatricality, very much of the opera house and of Italian opera in particular, with plentiful use of piccolo, a very distinctive role for solo trumpet, and even the solo cello from the opening of Rossini's *William Tell* overture. Listen carefully, however, to the triumphant brass chorale that closes the work (and first appears a couple of minutes in). Beginning with three repeated notes, it's classic Dvořák. In fact, it's nothing less than the trio of the First Symphony's third movement!

The title of *In Nature's Realm,* on the other hand, is self-explanatory: the work represents the apotheosis of all of the composer's pastoral mood pictures. He was a master of the genre, possibly the greatest ever. This work is also important because it introduces, at its opening, the motto that runs through the ensuing two pieces. Here it functions as the main theme, while in *Carnival* and *Othello* the motto is a subsidiary motive. The scoring is singularly light and airy: no bass drum; cymbals used sparingly but with plenty of triangle. In keeping with the rustic atmosphere, the genteel sounds of the harp are absent, but the woodwinds are very prominent, including the reedy sounds of English horn and bass clarinet. The only reason conductors seldom play *In Nature's Realm* is because, despite its overall radiance and verve, it commits one very serious crime: it ends quietly.

Carnival has long stood as one of Dvořák's most popular works, understandably. The music is brilliant, a blast to play, and a joy to hear. The English horn solo in its calm central interlude represents the essence of instrumental poetry, and the tambourine part remains a challenging test for any percussionist. *Othello,* unlike its two more genial partners, is intensely passionate, and it's just as fabulously scored. It makes a thrilling culmination to the cycle. Although some have tried to portray the piece as a narrative symphonic poem, noting the presence of Wagner's "magic sleep" motive from *Die Walküre* and claiming it represents Desdemona retiring to bed before her murder, I would disagree—unless of course she goes to sleep twice, for that's how many times this sequence appears. If you know the play, then it will come as no surprise that *Othello* describes musically the corrupting power of jealousy, symbolized by the warped, sinister reappearance of the "nature" motive on muted horns backed by suspended cymbals. The music has tremendous sweep and momentum, with the closing pages absolutely thrilling in their impetuosity.

Few pieces by Dvořák have staged such an impressive comeback in recent years as have the four great symphonic poems based on Czech folk-poems. From being almost universally derided, they are now rightly seen as belonging among his finest and certainly most progressive works. Two factors were instrumental in this change of perspective. The first was the recognition of the genius of Leoš Janáček, who loved these pieces, praised them in print, premiered two, and saw in them the origins of his own style of composition: that of creating melodies from the natural rhythms of speech. For Dvořák did more than just follow the stories closely; he based his tunes on the actual poetic verses, which fit whole sections of the music despite the fact that each work also has its own satisfying overall form. That was, and remains, an extraordinary achievement, as Janáček himself pointed out at the time.

The second factor leading to the rehabilitation of this music is the softening effect of the intervening years. Specifically, the shock value of the actual stories has worn off, at least to some degree. Contemporary audiences and critics confronted the sight of Dvořák, music's ultimate "Mr. Nice Guy," setting tales of axe-murder, rape, infanticide, poisoning, and suicide with the same sort of horror a mother today might feel on learning that Disney studios had decided to give up animated children's films entirely in favor of pornography. The very prospect seemed unbelievable, and so the result must necessarily be a failure. It was no such thing, and the whole point in using stories that expressed extremes of horror and grotesquerie is that (as a glance at the orchestration chart on page 142 will show) they permitted Dvořák to stretch his instrumental palette to the maximum, employing an entire repertoire of new and unusual sounds, and reaching new heights of vividness. These works are also the proving grounds of his late operas, with their own equally fantastic subjects.

The most interesting of the four works in this respect is *The Wood Dove,* which describes a widow burying her husband, whom she has poisoned so as to be able to marry her lover. After the funeral, with its magnificent imitation of the woman's false lamentation (descending violins weeping crocodile tears), party music strikes up, and she celebrates her marriage to husband number 2. Outside, over the grave of her first husband, grows a tree, and on its branches sits a dove that coos day and night, a sound that she cannot get out of her mind and that greets her at every turn. This arouses pangs of guilt so violent that the woman at last kills herself in remorse by leaping into a river and drowning, leading finally to a transfigured ending in which the cooing dove and the tormented spirit of the murderess find peace at last.

Although Janáček conducted the premiere, Gustav Mahler led one of the first subsequent performances in Vienna. He nevertheless claimed to dislike the work, and no wonder! It contains almost as much of what might now be called typical Mahler as it does Dvořák, including a sleazy funeral march (with solo trumpet and "Salvation Army" percussion), offstage brass announcing the

impending wedding, and the spooky cooing of the dove evocatively allocated to harp and woodwinds. If Mahler didn't actually borrow these sounds in his slightly later Fifth and Seventh
Symphonies, the coincidence is remarkable all the same. It's easy
to imagine how appalled he might have been to discover that,
according to Dvořák, the funeral-march first movement of his
Fifth Symphony might well represent the hypocritical mourning
of a murderess, while the eerie harp-writing in the second movement of his Seventh Symphony actually embodies the stylized
cooing of a dove.

Mahler's entire radical conception of the symphony was based
to a large extent on universalizing these otherwise programmatic
and descriptive gestures, freeing them from their narrative and
illustrative roots. There was a difference, then, between Dvořák's
progressive tendencies and Mahler's, and this in turn also at
least partially explains why these pieces were neglected even by
some of those artists best placed to appreciate their qualities. But
beyond that, *The Wood Dove* is one hell of a piece of orchestration, perhaps the most refined and magical single movement that
Dvořák ever wrote, and that's really saying a lot.

The Noonday Witch is the simplest and shortest of the four
works, although its story may be the saddest. A child is making
mischief (humorously, to Beethoven's Fifth), and his mother
warns him to behave or the Noonday Witch will come for him.
He naturally ignores this advice. The witch appears and twice
demands the child. The mother refuses and leads the witch on
a mad chase. Cornered, she clasps the child to her as the noon
bell rings and the witch vanishes. Coming home for lunch, the
father discovers his wife and son unconscious on the floor; she
regains consciousness, but the child is dead, suffocated in his
mother's frantic embrace. The music ends with the witch's
demand for the child blasted out in the brass in tones of utmost

horror and despair, while the coda offers a last ironic reminder of her evil laughter.

This terrifying, cruelly forthright piece is no joke, certainly not coming from someone who had himself lost three of his own children. However, as in the case of such works as Mahler's *Kindertotenlieder* (Songs on the Death of Children), the music is captivating in its various moods as well as stunningly orchestrated (there's some particularly evocative writing for bass clarinet at the witch's initial appearance, for example). Its intensity and, in a good performance, gut-wrenching impact stem from the unflinching emotional accuracy with which Dvořák takes the listener through each element of the story, from the innocence of the opening right up to the grim turn to the minor key when both parents realize that their child is dead.

The Golden Spinning Wheel has the grossest story, but it's also the most purely entertaining of the four works (the happy ending certainly helps). Girl meets prince. They fall in love. Girl tells stepmother and identical-looking stepsister. They chop her to bits, keeping a few parts to make sure she stays chopped up (you never know). Evil stepsister joins prince at the palace, as planned, to celebrate their wedding. Holy hermit finds the body and trades pieces of a golden spinning wheel for the missing parts. He reassembles the girl and revives her. They show up at the castle, whereupon the spinning wheel magically tells everyone the whole story. A happy ending ensues.

The longest of the symphonic poems (about twenty-five-plus minutes), some conductors foolishly cut the three-fold body-part-trading sequence, which is a mistake because the music is evocatively literal (although happily not to the point where you know exactly which part is involved), subtly varied on each repetition, and it's only about four minutes in total. Like that of the Eighth Symphony, the piece's form is a sort of ongoing, evolving series of variations on a few simple ideas heard right at the beginning.

The piece remains underestimated today, largely because some take its fairy-tale atmosphere and narrative style way too seriously, assuming that all four of these works demand the same sort of treatment, when in fact they are highly varied in content and emotional demeanor. Despite its grim (or should I say Grimm?) elements, this piece is great fun, first and foremost. It requires a light touch in performance and should sparkle.

This leaves only *The Water Goblin,* which you can hear in its gorgeously gruesome twenty-minute entirety on CD 2, track 10. The music, which follows the outline of the original folk-poem exactly, illustrates each event in the story in turn:

Beginning: Woodwinds play a portrait of the Water Goblin in the form of a perky theme with three repeated notes, much like the finale of the Fourth Symphony and the last movement of the "American" Suite, although more spiteful and sinister.

1:47: A charming pastoral scene of domestic tranquility in which the young girl tells her mother (on the woodwinds) that she wants to go down the lake to do her laundry.

2:35: The mother warns her: the Water Goblin is about (ghostly muted violins are prominent here).

4:03: But the day is lovely, so she goes anyway (full strings again). Note the rhythm of the Water Goblin's theme on the timpani under the lyrical theme of the girl, foreshadowing the tragedy to come—the same combination happens at the climax of the Fourth Symphony's finale, scored exactly the same way. This whole section, beginning at 1:47, takes the form of a theme followed by three variations.

5:20: The Water Goblin spies his prey and collapses the bridge on which the girl is standing (crash on tam-tam, cymbals, and bass drum at 5:38), dragging her down to his home under the lake.

6:25: She laments her misfortune on the cellos—note the omnipresence of the goblin's theme in the accompaniment.

8:53: The birth of the baby goblin. (Dvořák cleverly uses only the first three repeated notes of the full Water Goblin's theme high on the horns—a baby goblin indeed!) Its mother sings a gentle lullaby on flutes and oboes.

11:12: Domestic troubles at the goblin's house, represented by alternating lyrical and violent episodes. The girl asks permission to see her mother. Reluctantly, the goblin agrees, on the condition that (a) she must return at the agreed-upon time and (b) she must leave the baby as a pledge of her good faith.

13:26: Tender dialogue between mother and daughter (cellos vs. flute in a brief recapitulation of their original melody from the beginning of the piece).

14:55: Time's up. The music on the lower strings is exactly the same as opens the "Dead-House" scene in *The Specter's Bride* (CD 2, track 4), save for the addition here of the tam-tam. The theme of the Water Goblin returns, with lower strings illustrating his impatient circling about. After the church bell sounds (at 15:50), a storm brews over the lake, and the goblin pounds on the door with the three notes of his theme (16:10), again as in the vocal work. Notice, however, that because there are no words, the pounding on the door has significance both as a concrete image and also a reminder of the motive of the baby left behind. This is what good symphonic poetry is all about: making musical sense while also illustrating the details of the story.

17:14: In a fury, the goblin kills the baby and flings the corpse against the door (17:30). The work ends with a slow lament recalling the mother's warning (on English horn and bass clarinet), but the theme of the Water Goblin has the last word. This coda, and the Water Goblin's theme as well, bear a very striking resemblance to an important and very well-known early work of Sibelius: the symphonic poem *En Saga,* actually composed three years prior (Dvořák would not have known it, although he did meet the Finnish composer sometime later).

Dvořák's final symphonic poem, *The Hero's Song,* marks a fitting end to his orchestral output, as well as an apt conclusion to any book about him. The subject is non-narrative, and you may have been able to predict this merely from looking at the orchestration. Although the suspended cymbals remain, gone are the harp, any unusual percussion, and the nonstandard woodwind instruments. Instead the piece opposes two simple, basic moods: the despair of a funeral procession (with some wonderfully grinding dissonances) and unabashed triumph. The sheer physical energy of the piece is extraordinary, the tunes top-drawer. Mahler conducted the premiere, doubtless with a greater sense of relief than he felt on his initial encounter with *The Wood Dove.* There's little Mahler here—well, maybe just a bit in that funeral march—instead, an uninhibited outpouring of joyous energy that, no matter how loud the piece gets, offers the very opposite of posturing and pomposity. It is the sound of confidence.

Afterword

If, having come this far, I had to summarize Dvořák's essence for you in the simplest terms, I would point to a pair of recurring melodic archetypes running through his music from start to finish. The first of these is birdsong, symbolic of natural beauty, innocence, tranquility, God's handiwork, and therefore permanence. Second, there is the locomotive, those "train tunes," suggestive of progress, evolution, forward movement, and energy shaped by mankind's creative genius. For Dvořák, these images were not mutually antipathetic but related, as is a foundation to the building that it supports. Both were necessary for him: knowing who he was and where he came from, and using this knowledge as the basis for setting out on the grand adventure that constitutes his musical legacy.

Dvořák was also a *giver,* unstinting in his generosity and therefore a genuinely nurturing figure. His natural curiosity, freedom from prejudice, and lack of harmful inhibitions breathed fresh life into virtually every medium that he touched, and legitimized as no other composer before him the right of artists everywhere to pour new, indigenous, or ethnic musical wine into the most revered classical bottles. His reliability and versatility, the seeming ease with which he succeeded and the attractiveness of the results, ensured that he would be taken for granted— unfortunately, to the point where too much of his music has been condescendingly dismissed or simply neglected. This is more than a pity, because however important he may have been for broader cultural reasons in his own day, to his own country, and to the generations of composers inspired by his example that followed similar paths, the one fact that must never be forgotten is that Dvořák was, above all, a very great composer.

I began this book intending to limit it to a "best of" selection and wound up covering more than ninety individual works. Not all of them are equally important or fine, but there's amazingly little that does not reward your time and attention. Even Dvořák's weakest or most imitative pieces invariably sound like *someone,* rather than just *anyone,* a testament to his fundamental strength of personality. Most important, a huge quantity of music by any measure deserves to be considered extraordinary. I cannot think of another composer after Beethoven who demonstrated Dvořák's scope and productivity while maintaining such a high standard of overall quality. There's no surer bet in all of music, nor, when all is said and done, is there any body of work more melodically ravishing.

Appendix
Listening Lists

The following twelve short lists, containing five pieces each, suggest various angles of approach to Dvořák's dauntingly large output. I have not tried to list all the works that belong in each category or to cover all the possible categories, nor do I offer further discussion as to why the various works fit under each heading, as this would merely repeat comments made elsewhere in the initial discussions of each of them. Should you be curious, you can refer back to the appropriate chapter for a fuller explanation. I hope that you will find these selections useful, as a way of getting started and, more importantly, crossing the boundaries between genres to get a sense of why all this music sounds like Dvořák and no one else. Enjoy!

The Classical Tradition
Symphony No. 7
Piano Trio No. 3 in F Minor
String Quartet No. 13
Piano Quartet No. 2 in E-flat
Theme and Variations, Op. 36, for solo piano

The Master of Pastoral Music

Symphony No. 2
Symphony No. 5
Symphony No. 8
Czech Suite
In Nature's Realm

Dvořák and Wagner

Dramatic Overture
Othello Overture
Symphony No. 3
Symphony No. 4
The Devil and Kate

Dvořák the Progressive

Symphonic Variations
Scherzo Capriccioso
Symphony No. 8
The Wood Dove
Requiem

Slavonic Works

Slavonic Dances
Slavonic Rhapsodies Nos. 1 through 3
String Quartet No. 10
Piano Quintet No. 2 in A Major
"Dumky" Trio

American Works

Symphony No. 9 ("From the New World")
Cello Concerto
String Quintet No. 3, Op. 97
Humoresques, for piano
String Quartet No. 12 ("American")

The Quintessential Spirit of Dvořák

The Jacobin
Symphony No. 8
Scherzo Capriccioso
The Specter's Bride
Biblical Songs

Neglected-but-Really-Worthwhile (A Personal Selection)

String Quartet No. 4
Symphony No. 3
Piano Concerto
Symphonic Poem (Rhapsody) in A Minor, Op. 18
String Quartet No. 1

Charmers

Serenade for Strings
Serenade for Winds
Czech Suite
Cypresses, for string quartet
Legends

Surprising Masterpieces

Requiem
Dimitrij
Poetic Tone Pictures, for piano
String Quintet No. 2 in G ("Double Bass")
Bagatelles, for string trio and harmonium

Fabulous Musical Fairy Tales

Rusalka
The Devil and Kate
The Noonday Witch
The Golden Spinning Wheel
The Water Goblin

Dvořák, Brahms, and Brahms's Circle

String Quartet No. 9
Symphony No. 6
Symphony No. 7
String Quartet No. 11
Violin Concerto

CD Track Listing

The CD's contents are available for download at:
http://www.halleonardbooks.com/ebookmedia/331662

CD 1

1. Symphony No. 3 in E-flat Major, Op. 10: I—Allegro moderato (11:36)

   Václav Neumann, conductor, Czech Philharmonic Orchestra

   ℗ 1987 Supraphon
   From SU 3703-2 032

2. Symphony No. 6 in D Major, Op. 60: III—Scherzo (8:16)

   Charles Mackerras, conductor, Czech Philharmonic Orchestra

   ℗ 2004
   From SU 3771-2 031

3. Symphony No. 7 in D Minor, Op. 70: IV—Finale (9:17)

   Václav Neumann, conductor, Czech Philharmonic Orchestra

   ℗ 1981 Supraphon
   From SU 3705-2 032

4. Symphony No. 8 in G Major, Op. 88: II—Adagio (10:20)

   Václav Neumann, conductor, Czech Philharmonic Orchestra

   ℗ 1983 Supraphon
   From SU 3705-2 032

5. *The Devil and Kate*, Op. 112: Act 2—Overture (4:13)

   Jiří Pinkas, conductor, Brno Janáček Opera Orchestra

   ℗ 1981 Supraphon
   From 11 1800-2 612

6. *The Devil and Kate,* Op. 112: Act 2—Opening Chorus (1:48)

   Jiří Pinkas, conductor, Brno Janáček Opera Orchestra

   Josef Pančík, chorus master, Brno State Philharmonic Chorus

   Aleš Šťáva, bass

   ℗ 1981 Supraphon
   From 11 1800-2 612

7. *The Stubborn Lovers*, Op. 17: Lenka's Aria (3:25)

    Jiří Bělohlávek, conductor, Prague Philharmonia

    Zdena Kloubová, soprano

    ℗ 2004 Supraphon a.s.
    From SU 3765-2 631

8. *Dimitrij*, Op. 64: Xenia's Aria (5:48)

    Gerd Albrecht, conductor, Czech Philharmonic Orchestra

    Lívia Ághová, soprano

    ℗ 1991 Supraphon
    From SU 3793-2 633

9. *The Jacobin*, Op. 84: Serenade (Children's Chorus) (6:38)

    Jiří Pinkas, conductor, Brno State Philharmonic Orchestra

    Kantilena Children's Chorus

    Vilém Přibyl, tenor; Beno Blachut, tenor; Daniela Šounová-Brouková, soprano

    ℗ 1978
    From 11 2190-2 612

10. *Rusalka*, Op. 114: Song to the Moon (5:06)

    Václav Neumann, conductor, Czech Philharmonic Orchestra

    Gabriela Beňačková-Čápová, soprano

    ℗ 1984 Supraphon
    From SU 3717-2 631

11. String Quartet No. 14 in A-flat Major, Op. 105: I—Adagio ma non troppo—Allegro appassionato (8:03)

    Panocha Quartet: Jiří Panocha, first violin; Pavel Zejfart, second violin; Miroslav Sehnoutka, viola; Jaroslav Kulhan, cello

    ℗ 1986 Supraphon
    From 11 1459-2 131

12. Sextet for 2 Violins, 2 Violas, and 2 Cellos in A Major, Op. 48: III—Furiant (4:18)

    Panocha Quartet: Jiří Panocha, first violin; Pavel Zejfart, second violin; Miroslav Sehnoutka, viola; Jaroslav Kulhan, cello

    Josef Klusoň, second viola; Michal Kaňka, second cello

    ℗ 1992
    From 11 1461-2 131

CD 2

1. Trio for Piano, Violin, and Cello No. 3 in F Minor, Op 65: III—
Poco adagio (10:06)
Czech Trio: Josef Páleníček, piano; Alexander Plocek, violin; Miloš Sádlo, cello
Ⓟ 1951

2. Humoresques, Op. 101: No. 4—Poco andante (2:39)
Radoslav Kvapil, piano
Ⓟ 1967
From SU 3399-2 111

3. String Quartet No. 12 in F Major ("American"), Op. 96: IV—
Finale (5:09)
Panocha Quartet: Jiří Panocha, first violin; Pavel Zejfart, second violin;
Miroslav Sehnoutka, viola; Jaroslav Kulhan, cello
Ⓟ 1996
From SU 3572-2 131

4. Bagatelles, for 2 Violins, Cello, and Harmonium, Op. 47: I—
Allegretto scherzando (2:56)
Jaroslav Tůma, harmonium; Panocha Quartet: Jiří Panocha, first violin;
Pavel Zejfart, second violin; Jaroslav Kulhan, cello
Ⓟ 1997
From 11 1452-2 131

5. *The Spectre's Bride*, Op. 69: Bass Solo with Chorus (4:21)
Jiří Bělohlávek, conductor, Prague Symphony Orchestra
Pavel Kühn, chorus master, Prague Philharmonic Choir
Ivan Kusnjer, bass-baritone
Ⓟ 1996
From SU 3091-2 231

6. Requiem, Op. 89: Offertorium (11:58)
Karel Ančerl, conductor, Czech Philharmonic Orchestra
Markéta Kühnová, chorus master, Prague Philharmonic Choir
Maria Stader, soprano; Sieglinde Wagner, contralto; Ernst Haefliger, tenor;
Kim Borg, bass
Ⓟ 1959 Supraphon
From SU 3673-2 212

7. Slavonic Dances, Series II, Op. 72: No. 5 in B-flat Minor,
   Poco adagio (2:44)
   Karel Šejna, conductor, Czech Philharmonic Orchestra
   ℗ 1960 Supraphon
   From SU 1916-2 011

8. *Legends*, Op. 59: No. 6 in C-sharp Minor—Allegro con moto (5:16)
   Charles Mackerras, conductor, Czech Philharmonic Orchestra
   ℗ 2002
   From SU 3533-2 031

9. Scherzo Capriccioso, Op. 66 (14:08)
   Charles Mackerras, conductor, Czech Philharmonic Orchestra
   ℗ 2002
   From SU 3533-2 031

10. *The Water Goblin*, Op. 107 (19:45)
    Václav Neumann, conductor, Czech Philharmonic Orchestra
    ℗ 1978
    From SU 0199-2 011